Winning Management

If you are a business owner, a department manager, or a supervisor, you can profit from studying this new version of the ancient guide to success. For over 2,500 years, *The Art of War* has helped people like you find the path to victory.

As interpreted in *The Art of Management,* you can easily apply Sun Tzu's immortal ideas to modern decision-making. *The Art of Management* gives you Sun Tzu's lessons in a form that deals with employees, productivity, and the struggle for continuous improvement. *The Art of War & The Art of Management* together offer you a proven, workable approach to addressing the problems of running an organization in a competitive world.

The author, Gary Gagliardi, is a highly successful entrepreneur who used Sun Tzu's ancient wisdom to build a multimillion-dollar software company. He has written a number of books based on *The Art of War,* applying its lessons to sales and marketing. In this new work, he uses these ideas to address the most difficult struggle of all, the management of people.

Buy it today and study it forever!

Books for the Art of Business

Other Books from Clearbridge Publishing

The Art of War: In Sun Tzu's Own Words
The Art of War & The Art of Sales
The Art of War & The Art of Marketing

The Art of War
&
The Art of Management

孫
子
兵
法

Dedicated to my sister, Michele

THE ART OF WAR

&

THE ART OF MANAGEMENT

BY
SUN TZU
AND
GARY GAGLIARDI

CLEARBRIDGE PUBLISHING

Published by
Clearbridge Publishing

FIRST EDITION
Copyright 2000 © Gary Gagliardi

All rights reserved. No part of this book may be reproduced or transmitted in any part for or by any means, electronic or mechanical, including photocopying, recording, or by any information storage and retrieval system, without the written permission of the Publisher, except where permitted by law.

Clearbridge Publishing and its logo, a transparent bridge, are the trademarks of Clearbridge Publishing,

Manufactured in the United States of America
Front Cover Art by Gary Gagliardi
Back Cover photograph by Davis Freeman

Library of Congress Card Number: 00-100175
ISBN 1-929194-05-6
Clearbridge Publishing books may be purchased for business, for any promotional use, or for special sales. Please contact:

Clearbridge PUBLISHING
P.O Box 7055, Shoreline, WA 98133
Phone: (206)-533-9357 Fax: (206)-546-9756
www.clearbridge.com
info@clearbridge.com

Contents

Foreword ix

The Art of War &
The Art of Management

1. Planning 2
   - Analysis 3
2. Going to War 12
   - Decision Making 13
3. Planning an Attack 20
   - Attacking Problems 21
4. Positioning 28
   - Innovation 29
5. Momentum 36
   - Vision 37
6. Weakness and Strength 44
   - Problems and Opportunities 45
7. Armed Conflict 56
   - Competition 57
8. Adaptability 66
   - Continuous Improvement 67
9. Armed March 72
   - Making Progress 73
10. Field Position 88
    - Best Practices 89
11. Types of Terrain 102
    - The Work Environment 103
12. Attacking with Fire 124
    - Attacking Cycle Time 125
13. Using Spies 132
    - Acquiring Information 133

Foreword

You are holding my fourth and final book based on Sun Tzu's *The Art of War*. For over two thousand years, people have treasured this famous work. Today, most readers are like you, not military men but managers and business people looking for guidance to help them make better decisions. In this series of books, I have tried to apply Sun Tzu's lessons to our daily struggle for success in the modern world of organizations.

You may just be discovering Sun Tzu for the first time, or you may be looking for ways to more easily use his ideas. I discovered *The Art of War* over twenty years ago when I was working as a young sales person. From my first reading, it was clear that Sun Tzu's ideas on organization and competition worked in the modern world. His methods helped me find success, and they can help you as well.

These lessons take you where you want to go. In my case, I started my own software company after a successful career in sales and sales management. Since I'd found the ancient text so helpful personally, I rewrote it to train my sales staff in a book that I called *The Art of Sales*. Our sales people re-

The Art of War & The Art of Management

ceived it so well that I resolved to someday take the lessons of Sun Tzu to a broader audience of people like you.

As managers, you have to face a wide variety of issues. As the head of a fast-growing company, Sun Tzu's lessons helped me make better decisions. This management adaptation of Sun Tzu's work specifically addresses the problems of leading people, making decisions, and of process improvement. As in all our books, we give you this management version side-by-side with a complete translation of the original text of *The Art of War*.

As the first military classic, *The Art of War* offers you a distinct, non-intuitive philosophy on how to succeed. This philosophy realizes that certain key factors influence the outcome of any of your endeavors and that success goes—not to the strongest or most aggressive—but to the person who best understands the true situation and what the alternatives are.

In this management version, you get an adaptation tailored to help you in your role as an executive decision-maker. You will find that Sun Tzu's lessons work well for both the private and the public sector. They work for middle management and for top management. Since I had already written specific interpretations for sales and marketing, in this work I concentrated on handling employees, making decisions, improving the organization, time-management, creating a good work environment, and so on.

Why should Sun Tzu's philosophy of warfare apply so well to the problems of management? Sun Tzu was primarily a manager, concerned about using groups of people effectively. He wrote about human nature, innovation, and the struggle for success. Human organizations haven't changed in the last two thousand years and won't over the next two thousand. The only difference between modern organizations and ancient military ones are the types of tools and the battleground.

Some don't see how anything as horrible as war can teach us useful lessons in modern organization. More specifically, people see war as an adversarial, destructive process, while modern organization is a cooperative, productive activity. My response is to suggest that these critics read Sun Tzu's work. He did not see warfare as simply a matter of killing the enemy and destroying resources. His goal was psychological, convincing his people to fight and the enemy to surrender without a fight. He, more than anyone else, was familiar with the destructive nature of war. He did not teach blood lust. He taught the art of persuasion and organization as an alternative to destruction.

This approach works equally well in the modern world. I owe a debt of gratitude to the teachings of Sun Tzu. His lessons helped me throughout my career in management, and they will help you. Adapting his principles, we built our software company into a multimillion-dollar business, doubling in size every few years. From Sun Tzu, I learned how to analyze situations, innovate procedures, and inspire my fellow workers. Within five years, this approach allowed our product to become the number one accounting software in our market. These lessons can help you find similar success.

When we sold our software company, I wanted to bring the wisdom of Sun Tzu to a wider audience of people like you that might not normally study Chinese or military philosophy. I reworked my original *The Art of Sales* and published it as

The Art of War & The Art of Sales. I then created the marketing version, *The Art of War & The Art of Marketing*. Now I finish the job with this final volume, *The Art of War & The Art of Management*. All three of these volume are now available to help you apply Sun Tzu's lessons to modern competition.

As you get more deeply involved with studying Sun Tzu, you may want to know more about the original work. This is what happened to me. In doing my research, I discovered that the existing translations disagreed on Sun Tzu's meaning at essential points. This confusion forced me to go back to the Chinese ideograms to interpret faithfully his ideas. In the end, I created a new translation of the original text of *The Art of War.* You get this translation along with each of our books.

If you are interested in the original Chinese ideograms, my research led to the creation of a character-by-character translation of *The Art of War*. You can see these original Chinese phrases in the book, *The Art of War: In Sun Tzu's Own Words,* also published by Clearbridge Publishing. In it, the original ideograms are translated one at a time from the original phrases of Sun Tzu. The English sentence translation in this book results from that work.

You get both *The Art of War* and the adaptation, *The Art of Management,* side-by-side in this book. I encourage you to read both at the same time. As you are reading this work, notice how closely *The Art of Management* follows Sun Tzu's original concepts in *The Art of War*. While *The Art of Management* applies Sun Tzu's ideas in ways that he would never have foreseen, it does so respecting the integrity of his original lessons. I truly don't offer you these management ideas as my own but as interpretations of Sun Tzu's approach to successful organization building. I follow his advice and admonitions as closely as possible, line-by-line.

The military generals to whom Sun Tzu addressed his work were among the world's first serious managers. Like them, the leaders of today's organizations must compete with one another to survive. We compete on productivity, not destructive capability, but the rules of organization are the same.

What made this interpretation so natural was Sun Tzu's economic view of warfare itself. Sun Tzu reflected on the costly nature of war. The secret to warfare, he concluded, is not just winning battles, but winning in a way that doesn't impoverish the nation. This insight led to his entire approach to war as an exercise in understanding, organization, positioning, and persuasion. You can use this same thinking in making your own organization successful.

In management, your purpose shouldn't be just to get the job done, but to do so as efficiently as possible. All organizations, even those in the public sector, compete for resources. Even as part of a larger organization, you only get financial support if you are more productive than alternative providers in the marketplace. The competitive environment gradually weeds out ineffective and inefficient organizations. Management is, in our era, competition between groups of people for the most productive use of resources. It may be less lethal than war, but it is no less serious in terms of the survival of your organization and the people that work for you.

You will find the lessons that emerge from Sun Tzu are intriguing when applied to management.

First, Sun Tzu teaches us that management is not enough. The goal is to innovate, to find a way to get the job done with minimum cost. In modern terms, the goal is to minimize your costs while maximizing your productivity. Since organizations are expensive, the goal is to work quickly and efficiently. The most essential ingredient to success is picking the battleground, or, in our management translation, innovation. He was concerned with using the terrain and resources to outmaneuver the enemy. His concerns translated extremely well into an argument for continuous, gradual improvement. Sun Tzu gives a formula for reasoning out your plan for success. You calculate what improvements will give you the greatest competitive advantage. Any innovations must be well worth their cost.

Next, his lessons are extremely specific about what to do in certain situations. He wants you to pay close attention to the details of your situation. He enumerates different situations, different environments, different types of problems, and how you should respond to them. Although Sun Tzu wrote 2,500 years ago about warfare, when translated to management, these detailed lists still look surprisingly complete. Their advice is useful to anyone analyzing their organization's conditions. People are people. Organization is organization. Success is success in every era.

Next, Sun Tzu offers his "cooperative" view of working in a competitive environment. In his view, you can not succeed through your own actions alone. You don't create a successful organization. You can defend your existing organization from weakness, but the competitive environment itself must provide the resources for innovation. The secret to your success is recognizing an opportunity when it presents itself. Management some times requires watchful patience. Sun Tzu felt that opportunities are always abundant. Every problem creates an opportunity. It just takes us time to see them.

Finally, Sun Tzu viewed competition as knowledge-intensive. He saw success going to the best-informed person. He even recognizes creativity as a special and important type of knowledge. In Sun Tzu, there is no substitute for good information. *The Art of War's* last chapter, "Using Spies" makes it clear how essential good information is. In the management translation, this chapter becomes simply "Acquiring Information**.**" These chapters make it clear that Sun Tzu understood the information economy. He clearly saves his most important message for last. He says outright that nothing is as important as acquiring good information.

Despite its relatively short length, this book contains a great deal more specific information than books on management two or three times the size. Personally, I have studied *The Art of War* for twenty years. I learn more about sales, marketing and management every time I read it. You will too.

Gary Gagliardi, 2000

Planning

This is war.
It is the most important skill in the nation.
It is the basis of life and death.
It is the philosophy of survival or destruction.
You must know it well.

Your skill comes from five factors.
Study these factors when you plan war.
You must insist on knowing the nature of:
1. Military philosophy,
2. The weather,
3. The ground,
4. The commander,
5. And military methods.

It starts with your military philosophy.
Command your people in a way that gives them a higher shared purpose.
You can lead them to death.
You can lead them to life.
They must never fear danger or dishonesty.

ANALYSIS

This is management.
It is the skill that creates an organization.
It is the basis of start-ups and shutdowns.
It is the theory of endurance and elimination.
You can learn management.

Five elements determine your ability to manage.
Study these elements when you plan an organization.
You must understand:
1. Management philosophy,
2. The use of time,
3. The contribution to value,
4. Leadership,
5. And the decision-making process.

Management begins with a philosophy.
When you manage people, you must give them a shared goal.
You can end their current jobs.
You can give them new work to do.
They must not feel threatened or used.

Next, you have the weather.
It can be sunny or overcast.
It can be hot or cold.
It includes the timing of the seasons.

Next is the terrain.
It can be distant or near.
It can be difficult or easy.
It can be open or narrow.
It also determines your life or death.

Next is the commander.
He must be smart, trustworthy, caring, brave and strict.

Finally, you have your military methods.
They include the shape of your organization.
This comes from your management philosophy.
You must master their use.

All five of these factors are critical.
As a commander, you must pay attention to them.
Understanding them brings victory.
Ignoring them means defeat.

Next is the use of time.
Time can be tracked closely or disappear.
It can be productive or wasted.
It includes understanding your cycle of activity.

Next is everyone's contribution to value.
It can be eventual or immediate.
It can be arduous or effortless.
It can be broad or limited.
Creating value determines your organization's existence.

Next is your leadership.
Develop everyone's foresight, self-reliance, and courage.

Finally, you have the decision-making process.
It determines how you build your organization.
Your management philosophy creates it.
You must master decision-making.

All five of these elements are necessary.
You must focus on them.
They will bring success.
Losing sight of them leads to failure.

The Art of War: Planning

You must learn through planning.
You must question the situation.

You must ask:
Which government has the right philosophy?
Which commander has the skill?
Which season and place has the advantage?
Which method of command works?
Which group of forces has the strength?
Which officers and men have the training?
Which rewards and punishments make sense?
This tells when you will win and when you will lose.
Some commanders perform this analysis.
If you use these commanders, you will win.
Keep them.
Some commanders ignore this analysis.
If you use these commanders, you will lose.
Get rid of them.

Planning gives you an advantage because it makes you listen.
Planning makes you powerful.
Planning makes it easy for you to kill the enemy.
Planning is power.
Planning creates advantages and controls power.

You must educate yourself by analyzing.
You must understand your organization.

You must ask:
What is the right management philosophy?
Which managers are skillful?
Which uses of time and resources are valuable?
Which kind of management structure will work?
What are your organization's strengths?
Which managers and workers are trained?
What salaries and incentives make sense?
This is why some organizations work and others don't.
Some managers do this analysis.
If you employ them, you will be successful.
Keep them.
Too many managers never perform this analysis.
If you hire these managers, your organization will fail.
Get rid of them.

Analysis creates opportunities by forcing you to look.
Analysis makes managers successful.
It makes it easy to outstrip the competition.
Analysis is power.
Analysis discovers opportunities and focuses your energy.

Warfare is one thing.
It is a philosophy of deception.

When you are ready, you try to appear incapacitated.
When active, you pretend inactivity.
When you are close to the enemy, you appear distant.
When far away, pretend you are near.

If the enemy has strong position, entice him away from it.
If the enemy is confused, be decisive.
If the enemy is solid, prepare against him.
If the enemy is strong, avoid him.
If the enemy is angry, frustrate him.
If the enemy is weaker, make him arrogant.
If the enemy is relaxed, make him work.
If the enemy is united, break him apart.
Attack him when he is unprepared.
Leave when he least expects it.

You will find a place where you can win.
Don't pass it by.

The Art of Management: Analysis

Management is one thing.
It is a way of creating impressions.

When you expect success, make it seem unlikely.
When everyone is busy, make their workload seem light.
When deadlines are near, make it clear that you have time.
When deadlines are distant, make them appear immanent.

If the organization is comfortable, challenge it.
When people are confused, make decisions for them.
When times are good, prepare for the bad.
If the organizational structure is working, don't change it.
If people are upset, focus their frustrations.
If workers are insecure, give them confidence.
If employees are easygoing, work them hard.
If groups are too dependent, break them apart.
Challenge people when they seem unready.
Celebrate when they least expect it.

You must find ways to excite and inspire people.
Never pass up an opportunity.

Before you go to war, you must believe that you can count on victory.
You must calculate many advantages.
Before you go to battle, you may believe that you can foresee defeat.
You can count few advantages.
Many advantages add up to victory.
Few advantages add up to defeat.
How can you know your advantages without analyzing them?
We can see where we are by means of our observations.
We can foresee our victory or defeat by planning.

Before you take control of any organization, you must know how you can make it successful.
You must appreciate its strengths.
Before taking control, you must avoid organizations that will fail.
You can see only their weaknesses.
Feeding strength makes you successful.
Combating weakness leads to failure.
How can you understand strength without analysis?
You must study the organization by observing it.
You can foresee success or failure by analysis.

GOING TO WAR

Everything depends on your use of military philosophy.
Moving the army requires thousands of vehicles.
These vehicles must be loaded thousands of times.
The army must carry a huge supply of arms.
You need ten thousand acres of grain.
This results in internal and external shortages.
Any army consumes resources like an invader.
It uses up glue and paint for wood.
It requires armor for its vehicles.
People complain about the waste of a vast amount of metal.
It will set you back when you raise tens of thousands of troops.

Using a large army makes war very expensive to win.
Long delays create a dull army and sharp defeats.
Attacking enemy cities drains your forces.
Long campaigns that exhaust the nation's resources are wrong.

DECISION-MAKING

Everything depends on your management philosophy.
Moving an organization requires thousands of decisions.
Each decision is tested thousands of times.
People require equipment and supplies.
They need external customers to support them.
Some internal and external needs always go unmet.
Organizations always consume all their resources.
People require time and energy in management.
You defend your decision even against your employees.
People always complain about how little they are paid.
The larger the organization you build, the more time you lose in managing it.

Running a large organization is costly and time consuming.
Delaying action dulls any organization and leads to failure.
Building complicated organizations drains your energy.
Decisions that deplete your organization's resources are wrong.

The Art of War: Going to War

Manage a dull army.
You will suffer sharp defeats.
Drain your forces.
Your money will be used up.
Your rivals multiply as your army collapses and they will begin against you.
It doesn't matter how smart you are.
You cannot get ahead by taking losses!

You hear of people going to war too quickly.
Still, you won't see a skilled war that lasts a long time.

You can fight a war for a long time or you can make your nation strong.
You can't do both.

You can never totally understand all the dangers in using arms.
Therefore, you can never totally understand the advantages in using arms either.

You want to make good use of war.
Do not raise troops repeatedly.
Do not carry too many supplies.
Choose to be useful to your nation.
Feed off the enemy.
Make your army carry only the provisions it needs.

Let your organization get soft.
You will then suffer hard losses.
Expend your resources.
You thereby eliminate your options.
As an organization weakens, its employees lose confidence in the future.
It doesn't matter how smart you think you are.
You can't build an organization by sacrificing success.

You can sometimes decide to act too quickly.
Still, the more you delay decisions, the more often you fail.

You can try to play it safe when you make decisions, or you can be successful.
You can't have it both ways.

You can never completely understand the consequences of any decision.
You can therefore never completely understand the potential in any decision either.

You want to make good use of your people.
Don't keep turning over your employees.
Find ways to minimize your expenditures.
Concentrate on creating value for your customers.
Your customers must support you.
Give your people only what they need to create value.

The Art of War: Going to War

The nation impoverishes itself shipping to troops that are far away.
Distant transportation is costly for hundreds of families.
Buying goods with the army nearby is also expensive.
These high prices also impoverish hundreds of families.
People quickly exhaust their resources supporting a military force.
Military forces consume a nation's wealth entirely.
War leaves households in the former heart of the nation with nothing.

War destroys hundreds of families.
Out of every ten families, war leaves only seven.
War empties the government's storehouses.
Broken armies will get rid of their horses.
They will throw down their armor, helmets, and arrows.
They will lose their swords and shields.
They will leave their wagons without oxen.
War will consume sixty percent of everything you have.

Because of this, the commander's duty is to feed off the enemy.

Use a cup of the enemy's food.
It is worth twenty of your own.
Win a bushel of the enemy's feed.
It is worth twenty of your own.

You can kill the enemy and frustrate him as well.
Take the enemy's strength from him by stealing away his supplies.

You cannot afford to run an organization that is too spread out.
Coordination becomes too costly.
Using your internal resources exclusively is also expensive.
You must continually work to reduce costs.
Failure comes from exhausting your resources supporting poor decisions.
Management decisions are what bankrupt a company.
Poor management can destroy even the most successful organization.

Poor management destroys hundreds of companies.
Bad decision-making destroys organizations.
Poor organizational structure depletes company resources.
Lack of resources forces you to abandon assets.
Your people will lose their faith and forget their abilities.
They will forget both production and maintenance.
The machinery of the organization will break down.
The organization's productivity depends on management.

Because of this, you must make sure that you run the organization profitably.

Take a dollar's worth of productivity today.
It is worth twenty dollars tomorrow.
Create a dollar's worth of customer's value today.
It is worth twenty dollars of future potential.

You must support the organization and build confidence.
You need to create more value in the marketplace than you consume.

The Art of War: Going to War

Fight for the enemy's supply wagons.
Capture their supplies by using overwhelming force.
Reward the first who capture them.
Then change their banners and flags.
Mix them in with your own to increase your supply line.
Keep your soldiers strong by providing for them.
This is what it means to beat the enemy while you grow more powerful.

Make victory in war pay for itself.
Avoid expensive, long campaigns.
The military commander's knowledge is the key.
It determines if the civilian officials can govern.
It determines if the nation's households are peaceful or a danger to the state.

The Art of Management: Decision-Making

You compete for resources against all other organizations.
Find what is undervalued in the external market and buy it.
Reward those who find the right products.
Put your name and logo on these products.
Mix internal and external products to increase their value.
Retain your customers by being successful.
This is what it means to compete in the marketplace while growing more powerful.

Make success pay for itself.
Avoid long, expensive projects.
Your management decisions are the key.
They determine whether or not you can lead.
Your decisions determine if your organization is productive or wasteful.

Planning an Attack

Everyone relies on the arts of war.
A united nation is strong.
A divided nation is weak.
A united army is strong.
A divided army is weak.
A united force is strong.
A divided force is weak.
United men are strong.
Divided men are weak.
A united unit is strong.
A divided unit is weak.

Unity works because it enables you to win every battle you fight.
Still, this is the foolish goal of a weak leader.
Avoid battle and make the enemy's men surrender.
This is the right goal for a superior leader.

ATTACKING PROBLEMS

Your organization requires management.
A united organization is successful.
A divided organization is unsuccessful.
A united department is effective.
A divided department is ineffective.
A united team is productive.
A divided team is wasteful.
Devoted employees are dependable.
Indifferent employees are undependable.
A united effort is exciting.
A divided effort is painful.

Unity works because it enables your organization to solve the problems it encounters.
This still doesn't make you a great manager.
Avoid creating problems, and accomplish your goals.
This is the right goal for a good manager.

The Art of War: Planning an Attack

The best policy is to attack while the enemy is still planning.
The next best is to disrupt alliances.
The next best is to attack the opposing army.
The worst is to attack the enemy's cities.

This is what happens when you attack a city.
You can attempt it, but you can't finish it.
First you must make siege engines.
You need the right equipment and machinery.
You use three months and still cannot win.
Then, you try to encircle the area.
You use three more months without making progress.
The commander still doesn't win and this angers him.
He then tries to swarm the city.
This kills a third of his officers and men.
He still isn't able to draw the enemy out of the city.
This attack is a disaster.

Make good use of war.
Make the enemy's troops surrender.
You can do this fighting only minor battles.
You can draw their men out of their cities.
You can do it with small attacks.
You can destroy the men of a nation.
You must keep your campaign short.

It's best to solve problems before they are created.
The next best is to untangle problems.
The next best is to solve problems.
The worst is to try a complete reorganization.

Look what happens when you completely reorganize.
It looks great as a plan, but it will not succeed.
First, you must reinvent the processes needed.
You need the right people and resources.
This can take months and creates more problems.
You try to work around the problems.
After more months of work, you still won't make progress.
Everyone involved gets impatient for results.
You then try to throw money at problems.
This undermines your credibility and effectiveness.
You are still unable to make progress.
This approach is a disaster.

Make good use of your management time.
Let your people abandon poor practices.
You can solve problems with minor changes.
You must lure people away from their entrenched positions.
You do this gradually, a little at a time.
You can overcome any opposition.
You must keep your goals simple.

The Art of War: Planning an Attack

You must use total war, fighting with everything you have.
Never stop fighting when at war.
You can gain complete advantage.
To do this, you must plan your strategy of attack.

The rules for making war are:
If you outnumber the enemy ten to one, surround them.
If you outnumber them five to one, attack them.
If you outnumber them two to one, divide them.
If you are equal, then find an advantageous battle.
If you are fewer, defend against them.
If you are much weaker, evade them.

Small forces are not powerful.
However, large forces cannot catch them.

You must master command.
The nation must support you.

Supporting the military makes the nation powerful.
Not supporting the military makes the nation weak.

Politicians create problems for the military in three different ways.
Ignorant of the army's inability to advance, they order an advance.
Ignorant of the army's inability to withdraw, they order a withdrawal.
We call this tying up the army.
Politicians don't understand the army's business.
Still, they think they can run an army.
This confuses the army's officers.

The Art of Management: Attacking Problems

Once committed to a solution, throw everything in it.
Never give up when tackling a problem.
You can always find a competitive advantage.
To do this, you must plan your approach to problems.

The rules for overcoming opposition to change are:
If you have ten times the support, go around the opposition.
If you have five times the support, attack the opposition.
If you have twice the support, divide the opposition.
If your support is equal, pick only battles you can win
If your support is weaker, avoid confrontations.
If your support is much weaker, outpace the opposition.

Unpopular ideas cannot generate broad support.
Nevertheless, broad opposition cannot stamp them out.

You must master management.
Your organization must support you.

Supporting its managers makes an organization strong.
Undermining its managers makes an organization weak.

Company politics create problems for managers in three different ways.
Ignorant of which tasks are impossible, others insist on them.
Ignorant of which tasks are necessary, they propose different priorities.
This is called hamstringing your management.
Company politics is the opposite of management.
Everyone has an opinion about what must be done.
This confuses everybody's priorities.

Politicians don't know the army's chain of command.
They give the army too much freedom.
This will create distrust among the army's officers.

The entire army becomes confused and distrusting.
This invites the invasion from many different rivals.
We say correctly that disorder in an army kills victory.

You must know five things to win:
Victory comes from knowing when to attack and when to avoid battle.
Victory comes from correctly using large and small forces.
Victory comes from everyone sharing the same goals.
Victory comes from finding opportunities in problems.
Victory comes from having a capable commander and the government leaving him alone.
You must know these five things.
You then know the theory of victory.

We say:
"Know yourself and know your enemy.
You will be safe in every battle.
You may know yourself but not know the enemy.
You will then lose one battle for every one you win.
You may not know yourself or the enemy.
You will then lose every battle."

Company politics are blind to management hierarchy.
They assumes all internal desires can be satisfied.
This makes everybody uncertain of their goals.

If your people are confused, you lose their trust.
This invites new conflicts in every quarter.
We say that a disorganized organization fails at success.

You must know five things to succeed.
Success comes from knowing what needs doing and what does not.
Success comes from handling large and small groups well.
Success comes from everyone sharing the same goals.
Success comes from turning problems into opportunities.
Success comes from good management and avoiding company politics.
You must learn these five things.
You then know the principles of success.

We say:
Know your supporters and your opponents.
You will be secure in every confrontation.
You can know your supporters but not your opponents.
Then, for every battle you win, you will lose another.
You may know neither your supporters nor your opponents.
You will then lose every battle.

Positioning

Learn from the history of successful battles.
Your first actions should deny victory to the enemy.
You pay attention to your enemy to find the way to win.
You alone can deny victory to the enemy.
Only your enemy can allow you to win.

You must fight well.
You can prevent the enemy's victory.
You cannot win unless the enemy enables your victory.

We say:
You see the opportunity for victory; you don't create it.

You are sometimes unable to win.
You must then defend.
You will eventually be able to win.
You must then attack.
Defend when you have insufficient strength to win.
Attack when you have more strength than you need to win.

INNOVATION

Learn from other successful organizations.
Your first actions should stop what doesn't work.
Study your competitors to emulate their best practices.
Internally, you can only prevent organizational failure.
Success comes from outperforming external competition.

You must produce.
You can keep up with your competitors.
You cannot surpass them unless they leave an opening.

We say:
You must *see* the opportunity for innovation not *create* it.

You cannot always surpass your competitors.
You must then avoid falling behind them.
You will eventually be in a position to surpass them.
Then you must act.
Keep up when you don't have the resources to innovate.
Innovate when you have the resources you need to succeed.

You must defend yourself well.
Save your forces and dig in.
You must attack well.
Move your forces when you have a clear advantage.

You must protect your forces until you can completely triumph.

Some may see how to win.
However, they cannot position their forces where they must.
This demonstrates limited ability.

Some can struggle to a victory and the whole world may praise their winning.
This also demonstrates a limited ability.

Win as easily as picking up a fallen hair.
Don't use all of your forces.
See the time to move.
Don't try to find something clever.
Hear the clap of thunder.
Don't try to hear something subtle.

Learn from the history of successful battles.
Victory goes to those who make winning easy.
A good battle is one that you will obviously win.
It doesn't take intelligence to win a reputation.
It doesn't take courage to achieve success.

You must defend your organization well.
Conserve your resources and tighten spending.
You must act decisively.
Innovate when the benefits are clear.

Keep yourself in business until you are certain you've found a better way.

⸻

Some managers have innovative ideas.
Yet they don't know how to implement them.
This shows a limited ability.

Others push their people to outperform the competition, and everyone praises these managers.
This also shows a limited ability.

Innovation increases productivity effortlessly.
It doesn't exhaust your people.
Watch for the time to change.
Don't try to be too clever.
Listen for what makes a big difference.
Don't imagine subtle improvements that aren't there.

Learn from the history of successful organizations.
Success goes to those who find an easier way.
A good innovation is one that will obviously succeed.
You don't have to be a genius to achieve success.
You don't have to risk the organization to improve it.

The Art of War: Positioning

You must win your battles without effort.
Avoid difficult struggles.
Fight when your position must win.
You always win by preventing your defeat.

You must engage only in winning battles.
Position yourself where you cannot lose.
Never waste an opportunity to defeat your enemy.

You win a war by first assuring yourself of victory.
Only afterward do you look for a fight.
Outmaneuver the enemy before the battle and then fight to win.

You must make good use of war.
Study military philosophy and the art of defense.
You can control your victory or defeat.

This is the art of war.
1. Discuss the distances.
2. Discuss your numbers.
3. Discuss your calculations.
4. Discuss your decisions.
5. Discuss victory.
The ground determines the distance.
The distance determines your numbers.
Your numbers determine your calculations.
Your calculations determine your decisions.
Your decisions determine your victory.

You want to improve productivity easily.
Avoid difficult reorganizations.
Act when your ideas will be accepted.
You will always succeed if you avoid failure.

You must invest only in what works.
Make sure your competitors cannot surpass you.
Never pass an opportunity to surpass your competitors.

You overcome opposition by first finding a better way.
Only then do you look for a confrontation.
Outmaneuver your competitors before confrontation and then beat them decisively.

You must use your management skills.
Study management philosophy and the art of innovation.
You alone determine your success or failure.

This is the art of management:
1. A discussion of problems,
2. A discussion of statistics,
3. A discussion of analysis,
4. A discussion of changes,
5. And a discussion of improvements.

The environment determines the problems.
Tracking problems determines the statistics.
These statistics determine your analysis.
The analysis determines what changes.
These changes determine innovation.

Creating a winning war is like balancing a coin of gold against a coin of silver.
Creating a losing war is like balancing coin of a silver against a coin of gold.

Winning a battle is always a matter of people.
You pour them into battle like a flood of water pouring into a deep gorge.
This is a matter of positioning.

Creating a winning organization means insisting that something better replaces what is good.
Organizational failure is a matter of accepting what is good enough instead of insisting on better.

Successful innovation always depends on people.
Changing practices must carry workers forward into the future.
This is a secret of innovation.

Momentum

You control a large army as you control a few men.
You just divide their ranks correctly.
You fight a large army the same as you fight a small one.
You only need the right position and communication.
You may meet a large enemy army.
You must be able to encounter the enemy without being defeated.
You must correctly use both surprise and direct action.
Your army's position must increase your strength.
Troops flanking an enemy can smash them like eggs.
You must correctly use both strength and weakness.

It is the same in all battles.
You use a direct approach to engage the enemy.
You use surprise to win.

You must use surprise for a successful invasion.
Surprise is as infinite as the weather and land.
Surprise is as inexhaustible as the flow of a river.

Vision

You manage a large organization the same as a small one.
You only need to organize people correctly.
You overcome major obstacles the same as small ones.
You only need the right ideas and communication.
You may encounter a huge roadblock.
You must be able to meet serious difficulties without risking failure.
You only need to be creative while doing what you know.
Innovation must increase your productivity.
Creative thinking can make problems disappear.
You must appreciate both opportunities and problems.

It is the same in all struggles.
Doing what you know makes you competitive.
You use creativity to find success.

You must use creativity to grow the organization.
Creativity is as endless as time and the environment.
Creativity is a never-ending river of human innovation.

The Art of War: Momentum

You can be stopped and yet recover the initiative.
You must use your days and months correctly.

If you are defeated, you can recover.
You must use the four seasons correctly.

There are only a few notes in the scale.
Yet, you can always rearrange them.
You can never hear every song of victory.

There are only a few basic colors.
Yet, you can always mix them.
You can never see all the shades of victory.

There are only a few flavors.
Yet, you can always blend them.
You can never taste all the flavors of victory.

You fight with momentum.
There are only a few types of surprises and direct actions.
Yet, you can always vary the ones you use.
There is no limit in the ways you can win.

Surprise and direct action give birth to each other.
They proceed from each other in an endless cycle.
You can not exhaust all their possible combinations!

Yesterday's failure becomes tomorrow's success.
You must get the most out of everyone's time.

You can encounter huge obstacles and still recover.
You must understand how everything changes over time.

There are only a few basic human actions.
Yet you can combine them any number of ways.
You can always find a better way to get the work done.

There are only a few basic steps in any process.
Yet you can mix them in unlimited ways.
You will never exhaust your ability to improve.

There are only a few different resources.
Yet you can always blend them.
You will never discover all the possible combinations.

You succeed with vision.
There are only a few ways you can change what you do.
Yet you can continually adjust what you do.
There is no limit to the ways you can improve.

Innovative and standard methods need each other.
You must use both and move from one to the other.
Using both, you can never run out of good ideas.

Surging water flows together rapidly.
Its pressure washes away boulders.
This is momentum.

A hawk suddenly strikes a bird.
Its contact alone kills the prey.
This is timing.

You must fight only winning battles.
Your momentum must be overwhelming.
Your timing must be exact.

Your momentum is like the tension of a bent crossbow.
Your timing is like the pulling of a trigger.

War is complicated and confused.
Battle is chaotic.
Nevertheless, you must not allow chaos.

War is sloppy and messy.
Positions turn around.
Nevertheless, you must never be defeated.

Chaos gives birth to control.
Fear gives birth to courage.
Weakness gives birth to strength.

You must control chaos.
This depends on your planning.
Your men must brave their fears.
This depends on their momentum.

Different technologies reinforce each other.
The possibility of change washes away obstacles.
This is vision.

An innovation becomes suddenly practical.
It will sweep through the marketplace.
This is timing.

You must invest only in successful advances.
Your vision must be inspiring.
Your timing must be precise.

Your vision creates pressure in the organization.
Your timing should release it productively.

Customers are complicated and confused.
Industries are uncertain.
Your decisions must create order.

Processes are ineffective and inefficient.
Innovation outmodes them.
Nevertheless, you must never be at a loss.

Your customer's confusion demands your clarity.
Your industry's uncertainty demands your confidence.
Your problems create your opportunities.

You must organize what is disorganized.
This depends on your analysis.
You must give your people confidence.
This depends on your vision.

You have strengths and weaknesses.
These come from your position.

You must force the enemy to move to your advantage.
Use your position.
The enemy must follow you.
Surrender a position.
The enemy must take it.
You can offer an advantage to move him.
You can use your men to move him.
You use your strength to hold him.

You want a successful battle.
To do this, you must seek momentum.
Do not just demand a good fight from your people.
You must pick good people and then give them momentum.

You must create momentum.
You create it with your men during battle.
This is comparable to rolling trees and stones.
Trees and stones roll because of their shape and weight.
Offer men safety and they will stay calm.
Endanger them and they will act.
Give them a place and they will hold.
Round them up and they will march.

You make your men powerful in battle with momentum.
This is just like rolling round stones down over a high, steep cliff.
Use your momentum.

You have both problems and opportunities.
They give rise to innovation.

You must put competitors at a disadvantage.
Use innovation.
The industry must follow you.
Publicize a new approach.
Your competitors must try it.
You must be competitive to attract customers.
You can use your people to attract them.
You use your dedication to keep them.

You want to be successful.
You must have a vision.
Do not just pressure your people to solve problems.
Leverage good people using your vision.

You must invent your vision.
Your people must innovate to overcome difficulties.
Everyone should work together seamlessly.
People work together because of their skill and training.
Offer people safety and they will stay with you.
Threaten them with danger and they will act.
Give them a standard that they can hold on to.
Give them incentives and they will move forward.

You make yourself powerful with vision.
You can ignite people's imagination like a dry field catching fire.
Use your vision.

Weakness and Strength

Always arrive first to the empty battlefield to await the enemy at your leisure.
If you are late and hurry to the battlefield, fighting is more difficult.

You want a successful battle.
Move your men but not into opposing forces.

You can make the enemy come to you.
Offer him an advantage.
You can make the enemy avoid coming to you.
Threaten him with danger.

When the enemy is fresh, you can tire him.
When he is well fed, you can starve him.
When he is relaxed, you can move him.

PROBLEMS AND OPPORTUNITIES

You must know your problems so that you can plan time to deal with them.
If you don't leave time to solve problems once and for all, management is difficult.

You want a successful organization.
Guide your people without creating opposition.

You can make people follow you.
Offer them an opportunity.
You can discourage opposition.
Create problems for them.

If your people are too comfortable, challenge them.
If your people are satisfied, make them hungry for more.
If your people are lethargic, get them moving.

Leave any place without haste.
Hurry to where you are unexpected.
You can easily march hundreds of miles without tiring.
To do so, travel through areas that are deserted.
You must take whatever you attack.
Attack when there is no defense.
You must have walls to defend.
Defend where it is impossible to attack.

Be skilled in attacking.
Give the enemy no idea of where to defend.

Be skillful in your defense.
Give the enemy no idea of where to attack.

Be subtle! Be subtle!
Arrive without any clear formation.
Quietly! Quietly!
Arrive without a sound.
You must use all your skill to control the enemy's decisions.

Advance where they can't defend.
Charge through their openings.
Withdraw where the enemy cannot chase you.
Move quickly so that they cannot catch you.

Change established procedures and roles gradually.
Quickly implement new unexpected systems.
You can create new procedures and roles quickly.
To do so, you must start with a clean slate.
You must cement the changes your make.
Make changes where there is no opposition.
You must establish processes that will last.
Organize them in ways that are impossible to reverse.

Be skilled in changing what doesn't work.
Work in areas where no one has a stake to defend.

Be skillful in protecting what does work.
Design procedures that can only move forward.

You must make changes subtly.
Don't let potential opposition know what you plan.
You must keep quiet.
Make decisions without a fuss.
You must be skilled in controlling people's perception.

Make decisions that people can't oppose.
Look for your openings.
Go in a direction where opposition has no interest.
Move quickly so that opposition cannot form.

I always pick my own battles.
The enemy can hide behind high walls and deep trenches.
I do not try to win by fighting him directly.
Instead, I attack a place that he must rescue.
I avoid the battles that I don't want.
I can divide the ground and yet defend it.
I don't give the enemy anything to win.
Divert him from coming to where you defend.

I make their men take a position while I take none.
I then focus my forces where the enemy divides his forces.
Where I focus, I unite my forces.
When the enemy divides, he creates many small groups.
I want my large group to attack one of his small ones.
Then I have many men where the enemy has but a few.
My large force can overwhelm his small one.
I then go on to the next small enemy group.
I will take them one at a time.

We must keep the place that we've chosen as a battleground
a secret.
The enemy must not know.
Force the enemy to prepare his defense in many places.
I want the enemy to defend many places.
Then I can choose where to fight.
His forces will be weak there.

You must always prioritize your problems.
Some problems are systemic.
You can't overcome them by attacking them directly.
Instead, find a new approach that turns them around.
Avoid confrontations that you cannot win.
You can divide the work and defend its reassignment.
Don't leave potential opposition anything to attack.
Distract opponents from seeing what you are up to.

Identify where the problems are before you move.
Focus on the weak places in your processes.
When you link processes, you unite your people.
Problems divide people and create small groups.
The pressure toward unity must outweigh divisiveness.
Focus on teamwork rather than the self-interest of the few.
A united team can sweep away small cliques.
After tackling one problem, go on to the next.
Tackle problems one at a time.

You must keep any big changes that you are planning a secret.
Keep potential opponents in the dark.
Bring up many possible problems and potential solutions.
Let people oppose changes that you do not plan to make.
You can then choose where you want to focus.
Opposition will be weak there.

The Art of War: Weakness and Strength

If he reinforces his front lines, he depletes his rear.
If he reinforces his rear, he depletes his front.
If he reinforces his right, he depletes his left.
If he reinforces his left, he depletes his right.
Without knowing the place of attack, he cannot prepare.
Without a place, he will be weak everywhere.

The enemy has weak points.
Prepare your men against them.
He has strong points.
Make his men prepare themselves against you.

You must know the battle ground.
You must know the time of battle.
You can then travel a thousand miles and still win the battle.

The enemy should not know the battleground.
He shouldn't know the time of battle.
His left will be unable to support his right.
His right will be unable to support his left.
His front lines will be unable to support his rear.
His rear will be unable to support his front.
His support is distant even if it is only ten miles away.
What unknown place can be close?

We control the balance of forces.
The enemy may have many men but they are superfluous.
How can they help him to victory?

If opposition builds in one area, it lessens in another.
If people want one thing, they sacrifice something else.
If they are adamant on some issues, they loosen up others.
If some things are important, people compromise elsewhere.
Not knowing your intentions, opposition cannot form.
Incite opposition elsewhere so you can move where needed.

All organizations have weaknesses.
You must prepare to minimize them.
All organizations have opportunities.
Make your people focus on leveraging them.

You must know exactly what your goals are.
You must time your decisions precisely.
No matter how difficult the situation, you can still succeed.

Potential opposition must not know the changes you plan.
They must never know the time you plan to move.
Opposition on different issues must not unite.
General opposition must not focus on one issue.
Productivity must not disguise weaknesses.
Weaknesses must not stop productivity.
People won't oppose changes that they don't expect.
How can unknown plans be opposed?

You decide the balance of emotion.
People may vaguely oppose doing what is needed.
How can they stop you from succeeding?

We say:
You must let victory happen.

The enemy may have many men.
You can still control him without a fight.

When you form your strategy, know the strengths and weaknesses of your plan.
When you execute, know how to manage both action and inaction.
When you take a position, know the deadly and the winning grounds.
When you battle, know when you have too many or too few men.

Use your position as your war's centerpiece.
Arrive at the battle without a formation.
Don't take a position.
Then even the best spies can't report it.
Even the wisest general cannot plan to counter you.
Take a position where you can triumph using superior numbers.
Keep the enemy's forces ignorant.
Their troops will learn of my location when my position will win.
They must not know how our location gives us a winning position.
Make the battle one from which they cannot recover.
You must always adjust your position to their position.

This is always true.
You must allow yourself to succeed.

Your problems may be overwhelming.
You can still solve them by avoiding confrontations.

When you plan your strategy, know the strengths and weaknesses of your analysis.
When you execute your plan, know what needs to be done and what can be left undone.
When you make a decision, know where success and failure lie.
When you move, know when you have too many or too few resources.

Use your practices as the focus of your plan.
Go into every situation with an open mind.
Avoid defending particular practices.
Then the opposition can't spread rumors against you.
Even the most adamant opponent can't counter you.
Make decisions that have the weight of the organization behind them.
Keep potential opposition in the dark.
Potential opposition should learn about your plan only after it has been accepted.
They should not see how you created the support you needed.
Implement your plan so that it cannot be subverted.
Always adjust your plan to weaken any opposition.

Manage your military position like water.
Water takes every shape.
It avoids the high and moves to the low.
Your war can take any shape.
It must avoid the strong and strike the weak.
Water follows the shape of the land that directs its flow.
Your forces follow the enemy who determines how you win.

Make war without a standard approach.
Water has no consistent shape.
If you follow the enemy's shifts and changes, you can always win.
We call this shadowing.

Fight five different campaigns without a firm rule for victory.
Use all four seasons without a consistent position.
Your timing must be sudden.
A few weeks determine your failure or success.

You must remain flexible in your decision-making.
Decisions can take any shape.
Avoid what is difficult and do what comes easily.
Your organization can take any form.
You must leverage opportunities and minimize problems.
Follow the shifts in situations in order to direct their flow.
Organization's skills overcome problems to find success.

You must avoid rigid plans and procedures.
Ideas have no consistent shape.
By following the shifts and changes in the situation, you can always succeed.
This is called opportunism.

Use new ideas; no standard approach is always successful.
Use every moment to invent new approaches.
You must make decisions quickly.
An instant can determine your success or failure.

Armed Conflict

Everyone uses the arts of war.
You accept orders from the government.
Then you assemble your army.
You organize your men and build camps.
You must avoid disasters from armed conflict.

Seeking armed conflict can be disastrous.
Because of this, a detour can be the shortest path.
Because of this, problems can become opportunities.

Use an indirect route as your highway.
Use the search for advantage to guide you.
When you fall behind, you must catch up.
When you get ahead, you must wait.
You must know the detour that most directly accomplishes your plan.

Undertake armed conflict when you have an advantage.
Seeking armed conflict for its own sake is dangerous.

COMPETITION

Everyone uses the art of management.
You get your mission from your external customers.
Then you put together your organization.
You must hire your people and buy resources.
You must always avoid mistakes in the competitive market.

Ignoring the reality of competition is disastrous.
Because of this, you must find new approaches.
You must turn old problems into new opportunities.

You must travel a different path to find success.
Your opportunism must guide you.
If you just follow others, you will always be behind.
If you are too far ahead, you must be patient.
You must improve on the methods of others to succeed in your plan.

You can survive in a competitive world if you have an edge.
Never take your ability to survive for granted.

You can build up an army to fight for an advantage.
Then you won't catch the enemy.
You can force your army to go fight for an advantage.
Then you abandon your heavy supply wagons.

You keep only your armor and hurry straight after the enemy.
You avoid stopping day or night.
You use many roads at the same time.
You go hundreds of miles to fight for an advantage.
Then the enemy catches your commanders and your army.
Your strong soldiers get there first.
Your weaker soldiers follow behind.
Using this approach, only one in ten will arrive.
You can try to go fifty miles to fight for an advantage.
Then your commanders and army will stumble.
Using this method, only half of your soldiers will make it.
You can try to go thirty miles to fight for an advantage.
Then only two out of three get there.

If you make your army travel without good supply lines, they will die.
Without supplies and food, your army will die.
If you don't save the harvest, your army will die.

You can try to use size as your competitive advantage.
Then you will be too slow.
You can try to push people as your competitive advantage.
Then you abandon good communication.

You can prepare yourself for battle and directly attack every mistake.
You can work your people day and night.
You can force people to compete against one another.
You can go to great lengths to develop a competitive edge.
Then the competition lures your managers and people away.
Your best people are the first to go.
Your weaker people then follow.
Only a small fraction of your efforts will be rewarded.
You can try to push your people for a competitive edge.
Still your managers and employees will stumble.
Using this method, only half your people will stay.
You can try to work your people for a competitive edge.
Only two out of three will be productive.

If you try to compete without good communication, your organization will fail.
Without ideas and information, your organization will fail.
If you don't keep good people, you will fail.

The Art of War: Armed Conflict

Do not let any of your potential enemies know of what you are planning.
You must stay with the enemy.
You must know the lay of the land.
You must know where the obstructions are.
You must know where the marshes are.
If you don't, you cannot move the army.
You must use local guides.
If you don't, you can't take advantage of the terrain.

You make war using a deceptive position.
If you use deception, then you can move.
Using deception, you can upset the enemy and change the situation.
You must move as quickly as the wind.
You must rise like the forest.
You must invade and plunder like fire.
You must stay as motionless as a mountain.
You must be as mysterious as the fog.
You must strike like sounding thunder.

Divide your troops to plunder the villages.
When on open ground, dividing is an advantage.
Don't worry about organization: just move.
Be the first to find a new route that leads directly to a winning plan.
This is the how you are successful at armed conflict.

Don't let your potential competitors know what you are planning.
You must keep up with the competition.
You must know the market for people and resources.
You must know where the historical problems lie.
You must know where others bog down.
If you don't, you cannot improve your organization.
You must use the experience of others.
If you don't, you won't discover a way to innovate.

You manage by packaging your innovations.
By packaging, you can get people to change.
By packaging, you can confuse competitors and eliminate limitations.
You must move quickly and lightly.
You must be above reproach.
You must go after and win customers.
You must be reliable and dependable.
You must be secretive about your plans.
You must do exactly what you say.

Your organization must specialize to win customers.
When markets are open, specialization is an advantage.
Don't tinker with organization; concentrate on customers.
Be the first to invent a new way to create value in the marketplace.
This is the how you succeed at competition.

The Art of War: Armed Conflict

Military experience says:
"You can speak, but you will not be heard.
You must use gongs and drums.
You cannot really see your forces just by looking
You must use banners and flags."

You must master gongs, drums, banners and flags.
Place people as a single unit where they can all see and hear.
You must unite them as one.
Then, the brave cannot advance alone.
The fearful cannot withdraw alone.
You must force them to act as a group.

In night battles, you must use numerous fires and drums.
In day battles, you must use many banners and flags.
You must position your people to control what they see and hear.

You control your army by controlling its emotions.
As a general, you must be able to control emotions.

In the morning, people's energy is high.
During the day, it fades.
By evening, people's thoughts turn to home.
You must use your troops wisely.
Avoid the enemy's high spirits.
Strike when they are lazy and want to go home.
This is how you master energy.

Experience in management tells us:
"You can give orders, but you will not be heard.
You must leverage communication tools.
You cannot know what people are doing just by looking.
You must use reports and measurements."

Use communication tools, reports, and measurements.
Make sure your people can all see and hear.
Coordinate them to work together.
Your best people should teach the others.
Your worst people should not be able to hide.
You must unite them into a single team.

Use frequent messages to keep close to distant employees.
Even when people are local, you must count and measure.
You must communicate everything that your people see and hear.

You create teams by controlling people's emotions.
As a manager, you must be able to channel emotions.

In the morning, everyone's enthusiasm is high.
During the day, enthusiasm fades.
By the end of the day, people want to go home.
You must use your people wisely.
Avoid creating resistance and opposition.
Introduce changes when people relax and want to go home.
This is how you master enthusiasm.

Use discipline to await the chaos of battle.
Keep relaxed to await a crisis.
This is how you master emotion.

Stay close to home to await a distant enemy.
Stay comfortable to await the weary enemy.
Stay well fed to await the hungry enemy.
This is how you master power.

Don't entice the enemy when their ranks are orderly.
You must not attack when their formations are solid
This is how you master adaptation.
You must follow these military rules:
Do not take a position facing the high ground.
Do not oppose those with their backs to wall.
Do not follow those who pretend to flee.
Do not attack the enemy's strongest men.
Do not swallow the enemy's bait.
Do not block an army that is heading home.
Leave an escape outlet for a surrounded army.
Do not press a desperate foe.
This is the art of war.

The Art of Management: Competition

Use discipline and wait for problems to arise.
Keep calm and expect difficulties.
This is how you master emotion.

Build your knowledge and await ignorant competitors.
Build your resources and await unequipped competitors.
Build your success and await needy competitors.
This is how you master power.

Do not invite organized competition.
You must not compete where others offer solid value.
This is how you master adaptation.
You must follow these management rules:
Do not make a decision against the trends.
Do not push those that have no other options.
Do not follow those who lead you on.
Do not fight the competition's strengths.
Do not believe everything you are told.
Do not block people from getting what they want.
Leave people a way to save face.
Do not attack people who are hungrier than you are.
These are the rules of management.

Adaptability

Everyone uses the arts of war.
As a general, you get your orders from the government.
You gather your troops.
On dangerous ground, you must not camp.
Where the roads intersect, you must join your allies.
When an area is cut off, you must not delay in it.
When you are surrounded, you must scheme.
In a life-of-death situation, you must fight.
There are roads that you must not take.
There are armies that you must not fight.
There are strongholds that you must not attack.
There are positions that you must not defend.
There are government commands that must not be obeyed.

Military leaders must be experts in knowing how to adapt to win.
This will teach you the use of war.

Continuous Improvement

Everyone uses management skills.
You take orders from your external customers.
You organize your people.
When you run into problems, you keep going.
Where interests intersect, you find partners.
When a situation leads nowhere, you get out of it
When problems surround you, you need new ideas.
When you are in a do-or-die situation, you must fight.
There are paths that you must avoid.
There are people that you don't want to oppose.
There are problems that you cannot attack.
There are positions that you cannot defend.
There are rules that you must break.

Great managers must be geniuses at knowing how to adapt to succeed.
This will teach you the use of management.

The Art of War: Adaptabiilty

Some commanders are not good at making adjustments to find an advantage.
They can know the shape of the terrain.
Still, they can not find an advantageous position.

Some military commanders do not know how to adjust their methods.
They can find an advantageous position.
Still, they can not use their men effectively.

You must be creative in your planning.
You must adapt to your opportunities and weaknesses.
You can use a variety of approaches and still have a consistent result.
You must adjust to a variety of problems and consistently solve them.

You can deter your potential enemy by using his weaknesses against him.
You can keep your enemy's army busy by giving it work to do.
You can rush your enemy by offering him an advantageous position.

Some managers are unable to change their approach to create an opportunity.
They might know the nature of their situation.
Still, they are unable to discover the hidden opportunity.

Some managers do not know how to change their methods of operation.
They can see an opportunity.
Still, they are unable to adapt so that they can use it.

You must continuously improve your analysis.
You must adapt to your opportunities and problems.
You can change your methods and still create consistent results.
You must tackle one problem after another and solve them once and forever.

You can discourage your opponents by using their weaknesses against them.
You can keep potential malcontents distracted by keeping them busy.
You can guide your opposition by giving them a goal to go after.

The Art of War: Adaptabiilty

You must make use of war.
Do not trust that the enemy isn't coming.
Trust on your readiness to meet him.
Do not trust that the enemy won't attack.
We must rely only on our ability to pick a place that the enemy can't attack.

You can exploit five different faults in a leader.
If he is willing to die, you can kill him.
If he wants to survive, you can capture him.
He may have a quick temper.
You can then provoke him with insults.
If he has a delicate sense of honor, you can disgrace him.
If he loves his people, you can create problems for him.
In every situation, look for these five weaknesses.
They are common faults in commanders.
They always lead to military disaster.

To overturn an army, you must kill its general.
To do this, you must use these five weaknesses.
You must always look for them.

You must make decisions.
You must never pretend that problems won't arise.
Instead, be ready to address unexpected problems.
Do not think that opposition won't arise.
Instead, you must prepare plans that are difficult to undermine.

All managers have five potentially fatal weaknesses.
If they can accept failure, they will fail.
If they are just trying to survive, they are trapped.
Some managers overreact.
They rush into making mistakes.
If they are afraid of criticism, they fail to decide.
If they are too fond of their people, they create problems.
In every situation, look for these five weaknesses.
They are common faults in many managers.
They can lead you to disaster.

These weaknesses can destroy you and your organization.
You must know how to avoid these weaknesses.
You must always be aware of them.

Armed March

Everyone moving their army must adjust to the enemy.

Keep out of the mountains and in the valleys.
Position yourself on the heights facing the sun.
To win your battles, never attack uphill.
This is how you position your army in the mountains.

When water blocks you, keep far away from it.
Let the enemy cross the river and wait for him.
Do not meet him in midstream.
Wait for him to get half his forces across and then take advantage of the situation.

You need to be able to fight.
You can't do that if you are in the water when you meet an attack.
Position yourself upstream, facing the sun.
Never face against the current.
Always position your army upstream when near the water.

MAKING PROGRESS

In every organization, you must serve the customer.

Avoid costly commitments and make small improvements.
Keep your organization visible and accessible.
To tackle problems, never throw money at them.
This is how to make progress in expensive situations.

When a technology will limit you, avoid it.
Let your competitors invest in it and use time against them.
Don't compete on who has the latest technology.
Wait until a technology is well proven and then take advantage of falling prices.

You need to be productive.
You can't if you are wrestling with technology instead of serving your customers.
Use technology to make your processes visible.
Never fight against technological trends.
Leverage the trends when implementing a technology.

You may have to move across marshes.
Move through them quickly without stopping.
You may meet the enemy in the middle of a marsh.
You must keep on the water grasses.
Keep your back to a clump of trees.
This is how you position your army in a marsh.

On a level plateau, take a position that you can change.
Keep the higher ground on your right and to the rear.
Keep the danger in front of you and safety behind.
This is how you position yourself on a level plateau.

You can find an advantage in all four of these situations.
Learn from the great emperor who used positioning to
conquer his four rivals.

Armies are stronger on high ground and weaker on low.
They are better camping on sunny, southern hillsides than on
the shady, northern ones.
Provide for your army's health and place it well.
Your army will be free from disease.
Done correctly, this means victory.

You must sometimes defend on a hill or riverbank.
You must keep on the south side in the sun.
Keep the uphill slope at your right rear.

This will give the advantage to your army.
It will always give you a position of strength.

You may have to implement a short-term solution.
Use it briefly and never leave it in place.
You will have problems with short-term solutions.
When you do, save what is working well.
Work toward a solid, long-term resolution.
This is how your make progress in the short-term.

When conditions are stable, identify what can be improved.
Invest in visibility and internal infrastructure.
Make problems visible and protect what works.
This is how to make progress in stable situations.

You can make progress in any situation.
Learn from successful managers who have continually improved their organizations.

Groups are stronger with cash and weaker without it.
You are better with solid, cash reserves than with forecasted budget surpluses.
Keep your organization healthy by keeping it solvent.
Your organization will be free from debt pressure.
Do this correctly, and you will be successful.

Sometimes you must take on debt.
Keep it minimal and keep it visible.
Use it to build infrastructure.

This will create opportunities for your organization.
Cash always gives you a position of strength.

The Art of War:: Armed March

Stop the march when the rain swells the river into rapids.
You may want to ford the river.
Wait until it subsides.

All regions have dead-ends such as waterfalls.
There are deep lakes.
There are high cliffs.
There are dense jungles.
There are thick quagmires.
There are steep crevasses.
Get away from all these quickly.
Do not get close to them.
Keep them at a distance.
Maneuver the enemy close to them.
Position yourself facing these dangers.
Push the enemy back into them.

Danger can hide on your army's flank.
There are reservoirs and lakes.
There are reeds and thickets.
There are forests of trees.
Their dense vegetation provides a hiding place.
You must cautiously search through them.
They can always hide an ambush.

Stop making changes when technological change is rapid.
You may want to use an evolving technology.
Wait until it stabilizes.

All organizations have boundaries that limit capacity.
There are resource limitations.
There are cost limitations.
There are information limitations.
There are legal limitations.
There are span of control limitations.
Always avoid these limitations.
Do not even get close to them.
Leave yourself plenty of capacity.
You want to limit only your problems.
Keep your eye on your problems.
Stretch your limited resources by eliminating problems.

Danger can hide at the edges of your organization.
Beware of habits and prejudices.
Beware of hidden assumptions.
Beware of established processes.
Complicated processes provide a hiding place.
You must examine everything carefully.
You don't want to be blind-sided.

Sometimes, the enemy is close by but remains calm.
Expect to find him in a natural stronghold.
Other times, he remains at a distance but provokes battle.
He wants you to attack him.

He sometimes shifts the position of his camp.
He is looking for an advantageous position.

The trees in the forest move.
Expect that the enemy is coming.
The tall grasses obstruct your view.
Be suspicious.

The birds take flight.
Expect that the enemy is hiding.
Animals startle.
Expect an ambush.

Notice the dust.
It sometimes rises high in a straight line.
Vehicles are coming.
The dust appears low in a wide band.
Foot soldiers are coming.
The dust seems scattered in different areas.
The enemy is collecting firewood.
Any dust is light and settling down.
The enemy is setting up camp.

Some problems happen frequently but are expected.
You must understand that they are well entrenched.
Other problems are uncommon but get attention.
Don't let them draw your resources.

Sometimes the source of a problem seems to shift around.
Solving it once and forever presents a real opportunity.

Well-established processes become less consistent.
Expect that a change has occurred.
Some processes are hard to measure.
Distrust them.

Customers start to leave.
Look for hidden problems.
Employees quit.
Expect unhappy surprises.

Notice expenses.
Expenses can rise quickly in a specific area.
A quick change is coming.
Expenses can rise generally across a broad area.
This means that the market is getting more competitive.
Cost increases can be scattered throughout the organization.
This means people are padding their budgets.
Expense increases can be slight and fall down again.
This means that you have problems under control.

The Art of War:: Armed March

Your enemy speaks humbly while building up forces.
He is planning to advance.

The enemy talks aggressively and pushes as if to advance.
He is planning to retreat.

Small vehicles exit his camp first and move to positions on the army's flanks.
They are forming a battle line.

Your enemy tries to sue for peace but without offering a treaty.
He is plotting.

Your enemy's men run to leave and yet form ranks.
You should expect action.

Half his army advances and the other half retreats.
He is luring you.

Your enemy plans to fight but his men just stand there.
They are starving.

Those who draw water drink it first.
They are thirsty.

Your enemy sees an advantage but does not advance.
His men are tired.

Birds gather.
Your enemy has abandoned his camp.

A problem can seem unimportant but keeps growing.
It will get serious.

People worry about a potential problem and prepare for it.
It will be minimal.

Sudden changes in the organization aggravate problems that already exist.
You must address them.

Some problems seem to fade a bit but never go away entirely.
They will arise later.

Some problems seem easily solved but reappear later.
You need to do more.

Don't solve problems only to create as many new ones.
This is a trap.

There are solutions that can't be implemented.
There are limits to resources.

Those installing systems tackle their own problems first.
This means everyone is needy.

There is an opportunity but people can't take advantage.
People are overworked.

Customers come.
This means that you are ahead of the competition.

Your enemy's soldiers call in the night.
They are afraid.

Your enemy's army is raucous.
They do not take their commander seriously.

Your enemy's banners and flags shift.
Order is breaking down.

Your enemy's officers are irritable.
They are exhausted.

Your enemy's men kill their horses for meat.
They are out of provisions.

They don't put their pots away or return to their tents.
They expect to fight to the death.

Enemy troops appear sincere and agreeable.
But their men are slow to speak to each other.
They are no longer united.

Your enemy offers too many incentives to his men.
He is in trouble.

Your enemy gives out too many punishments.
His men are weary.

Your enemy first attacks and then is afraid of your larger force.
His best troops have not arrived.

People only suggest improvement anonymously.
They are afraid.

Employees are undisciplined.
They don't take management seriously.

The organization is reorganizing and giving new titles.
Order is endangered.

Managers are short-tempered.
They are overworked.

The organization starts selling assets.
Operations are unprofitable.

People fail to put anything away or stay in their areas.
Expect them to resist changes.

People seem sincere and agreeable.
Nevertheless, they fail to communicate.
They do not see themselves as a team.

The organization must offer incentives to get work done.
It is in trouble.

The organization needs constantly to discipline its people.
It is under pressure.

Your opponents first attack you and then quickly tries to make friends.
They are developing more resources.

Your enemy comes in a conciliatory manner.
He needs to rest and recuperate.

Your enemy is angry and appears to welcome battle.
This goes on for a long time, but he doesn't attack.
He also doesn't leave the field.
You must watch him carefully.

If you are too weak to fight, you must find more men.
In this situation, you must not act aggressively.
You must unite your forces, expect the enemy, recruit men and wait.

You must be cautious about making plans and adjust to the enemy.
You must increase the size of your forces.

With new, undedicated soldiers, you can depend on them if you discipline them.
They will tend to disobey your orders.
If they do not obey your orders, they will be useless.

You can depend on seasoned, dedicated soldiers.
But you must avoid disciplining them without reason.
Otherwise, you cannot use them.

You must control your soldiers with *esprit de corp*.
You must bring them together by winning victories.
You must get them to believe in you.

Opponents suggest a compromise solution.
They are simply buying time.

People seem angry at changes and threaten to fight them.
They remain opposed but do what they are told.
Nevertheless, they never agree.
You must keep your eye on them.

If the work isn't getting done, you must hire more people.
However, you must not try to expand operations.
You must build your organization, train your new people, and be patient.

You must plan carefully and work continually to improve the organization.
You must increase the expertise of your team.

With new, untrained employees, you can depend on them if you tell them exactly what to do.
Otherwise, they will get confused.
If they are confused, they cannot be productive.

It is different with established, trained employees.
You must let them see for themselves what needs doing.
If they can't, they aren't good employees.

You must lead your people by inspiring them.
You unite them by making them successful.
They must believe in you.

Make it easy for them to obey your orders by training your people.
Your people will then obey you.
If you do not make it easy to obey, you won't train your people.
Then they will not obey.

Make your commands easy to follow.
You must understand the way a crowd thinks.

Make it easy for people to follow directions by training them well.
They will then do what is necessary.
If operations are difficult to understand, you won't be able to train people.
Then they will make mistakes.

Make your processes easy to understand.
You must understand how groups of people work.

Field Position

Some field positions are unobstructed.
Some field positions are entangling.
Some field positions are supporting.
Some field positions are constricted.
Some field positions give you a barricade.
Some field positions are spread out.

You can attack from some positions easily.
Others can attack you easily as well.
We call these unobstructed positions.
These positions are open.
On them, be the first to occupy a high, sunny area.
Put yourself where you can defend your supply routes.
Then you will have an advantage.

Best Practices

Some processes are open.
Some processes are entangling.
Some processes are best practices.
Some processes are proprietary.
Some processes create protective barriers.
Some processes are too slow.

You can improve some of your practices easily.
Problems can arise from these changes as well.
These are open processes.
These processes present no obstacles to improvement.
With these procedures, keep their results highly visible.
Concentrate on keeping them working.
They are then valuable processes.

The Art of War: Field Position

You can attack from some positions easily.
Disaster arises when you try to return to them.
These are entangling positions.
These field positions are one-sided.
Wait until your enemy is unprepared.
You can then attack from these positions and win.
Avoid a well prepared enemy.
You will try to attack and lose.
Since you can't return, you will meet disaster.
These field positions offer no advantage.

I cannot leave some positions without losing an advantage.
If the enemy leaves this ground, he also loses an advantage.
We call these supporting field positions.
These positions strengthen you.
The enemy may try to entice me away.
Still, I will hold my position.
You must entice the enemy to leave.
You then strike him as he is leaving.
These field positions offer an advantage.

Some field positions are constricted.
I try to get to these positions before the enemy does.
You must fill these areas and await the enemy.
Sometimes, the enemy will reach them first.
If he fills them, do not follow him.
But if he fails to fill them, you can go after him.

You can improve some processes easily.
You cannot return to old methods after making changes.
These are entangling processes.
They give you one chance.
Wait until you are certain a new procedure will work.
You can then replace an entangling process successfully.
Avoid lack of preparation.
You can launch a new process and have it fail.
Since you can't go back, you create a nightmare.
These processes are problems.

You cannot improve some practices.
Your competitors cannot improve on them either.
These are the best current processes.
The processes create value.
You may be tempted to try to change them.
You must keep them in place.
Let your competitors experiment with them.
You can then attack your competiors for changing.
These practices offer a clear advantage.

Some practices are proprietary.
You must patent them before the competition does.
You must protect yourself and await a challenge.
Your competitors may use them first.
If they protect these processes, don't try to copy them.
If competitors leave you an opening, you can copy them.

The Art of War: Field Position

Some field positions give you a barricade.
I get to these positions before the enemy does.
You occupy their southern, sunny heights and wait for the enemy.
Sometimes the enemy occupies these areas first.
If so, entice him away.
Never go after him.

Some field positions are too spread out.
Your force may seem equal to the enemy.
Still you will lose if you provoke a battle.
If you fight, you will not have any advantage.

These are the six types of field positions.
Each battleground has its own rules.
As a commander, you must know where to go.
You must examine each position closely.

Some armies can be outmaneuvered.
Some armies are too lax.
Some armies fall down.
Some armies fall apart.
Some armies are disorganized.
Some armies must retreat.

Know all six of these weaknesses.
They lead to losses on both good and bad ground.
They all arise from the army's commander.

Some processes create protective barriers.
You must establish these processes before competitors do.
You then must promote your procedures and await competitive attacks.
Sometimes competitors establishes these processes first.
If so, wait for your competitors to change
Do not duplicate these processes.

Some practices are too slow.
Your resources may be equal to those of your competitors.
Nevertheless, you will lose in a battle.
In competitive markets, slow cycles offer no advantage.

These are the six categories of procedures.
Each organization has its own methods.
As a manager, you must know your practices.
You must analyze each procedure carefully.

Some organizations can be outmoded.
Some organizations are stagnant.
Some organizations stumble.
Some organizations self-destruct.
Some organizations are chaotic.
Some organizations must downsize.

You must recognize these six weaknesses.
These problems arise in good conditions and bad.
Your decisions create them.

The Art of War: Field Position

One general can command a force equal to the enemy.
Still his enemy outflanks him.
This means that his army can be outmaneuvered.

Another can have strong soldiers, but weak officers.
This means that his army will be too lax.

Another has strong officers but weak soldiers.
This means that his army will fall down.

Another has sub-commanders that are angry and defiant.
They attack the enemy and fight their own battles.
As a commander, he cannot know the battlefield.
This means that his army will fall apart.

Another general is weak and easygoing.
He fails to make his orders clear.
His officers and men lack direction,
This shows in his military formations.
This means that his army will be disorganized.

Another general fails to predict the enemy.
He pits his small forces against larger ones.
He puts his weak forces against stronger ones.
He fails to pick his fights correctly.
This means that his army must retreat.

You must know all about these six weaknesses.
You must understand the philosophies that lead to defeat.
When a general arrives, you can know what he will do.
You must study each one carefully.

An organization may be competitive in the market.
Still, it lets itself fall behind.
These organizations will become outmoded.

Some employees are strong but have weak managers.
Their organizations will become stagnant.

Some managers are strong, but their employees are weak.
Their organizations will wear down.

Some managers are excitable and undisciplined.
They each have their own agenda.
The chief executive cannot know their true priorities.
Their organizations will self-destruct.

Some chief officers are lazy and sloppy.
They fail to make their priorities clear.
Their managers and employees lack direction.
This shows in the organization's lack of focus.
Their organizations are chaotic.

Some managers fail to understand the competition.
They pit weak processes against stronger ones.
They put poor practices against better ones.
They fail to pick their battles correctly.
Their organizations must downsize.

You must understand all six of these faults.
You must understand the thinking that creates them.
When you face these situations, you must know what to do.
You must study each one carefully.

The Art of War: Field Position

You must control your field position.
It will always strengthen your army.

You must predict the enemy to overpower him and win.
You must analyze the obstacles, dangers, and distances.
This is the best way to command.

Understand your field position before you go to battle.
Then you will win.
You can fail to understand your field position and still fight.
Then you will lose.

You must provoke battle when you will certainly win.
It doesn't matter what you are ordered.
The government may order you not to fight.
Despite that, you must always fight when you will win.

Sometimes provoking a battle will lead to a loss.
The government may order you to fight.
Despite that, you must avoid battle when you will lose.

You must advance without desiring praise.
You must retreat without fearing shame.
The only correct move is to preserve your troops.
This is how you serve your country.
This is how you reward your nation.

The Art of Management: Best Practices

You must control your processes and procedures.
Sound practices always strengthen your organization.

You must foresee problems and how to eliminate them.
You must analyze capacities, mistakes, and limitations.
This is the best way to manage.

You must make sure you are using the best practices.
Then you will succeed.
You may fail to use the best practices and try to compete.
Then you will fail.

You improve a process when you know you can fix it.
It doesn't matter what else needs doing.
The organization may have other priorities.
Still, you must always improve processes when you can.

Sometimes, you cannot change procedures successfully.
Your organization may desire a change.
Still, you must avoid changes that will not work.

You must make improvements without wanting praise.
You must abandon failures without embarrassment.
The only goal is to serve the customer.
This is how you serve your organization.
This is how you ensure success.

The Art of War: Field Position

Think of your soldiers as little children.
You can make them follow you into a deep river.
Treat them as your beloved children.
You can lead them all to their deaths.

Some leaders are generous, but cannot use their men.
They love their men, but cannot command them.
Their men are unruly and disorganized.
These leaders create spoiled children.
Their soldiers are useless.

You may know what your soldiers will do in an attack.
You may not know if the enemy is vulnerable to attack.
You will then win only half the time.
You may know that the enemy is vulnerable to attack.
You may not know if your men are capable of attacking them.
You will still win only half the time.
You may know that the enemy is vulnerable to attack.
You may know that your men are ready to attack.
You may not know how to position yourself in the field for battle.
You will still win only half the time.

You must know how to make war.
You can then act without confusion.
You can attempt anything.

Think of your employees as your children.
They will support you in difficult circumstances.
Train them with care and understanding.
They will serve you faithfully.

Some pay good wages but do not value their people.
They care about individuals but do not guide them.
Their employees are unhappy and confused.
These managers create bad employees.
Their people are useless.

You may know what your people do in your organization.
You must also know how they create value for customers.
If you don't, you have only done half your job.
You can know how to create value for the customer.
You must also know how to organize your people to create that value.
If you don't, you have only done half your job.
You can know how to create value for customers.
You can know how to organize your people to do it.
You must also know exactly how to formulate the processes in your organization.
If you don't, you have done only half your job.

You must know how to improve your practices.
You can then act with certainty.
You can compete anywhere.

We say:
Know the enemy and know yourself.
Your victory will be painless.
Know the weather and the field.
Your victory will be complete.

We repeat:
Know your competitors and your organization.
Then success will be effortless.
Understand people's thinking and your processes.
Then your success is assured.

Types of Terrain

Use the art of war.
Know when the terrain will scatter you.
Know when the terrain will be easy.
Know when the terrain will be disputed.
Know when the terrain is open.
Know when the terrain is intersecting.
Know when the terrain is dangerous.
Know when the terrain is bad.
Know when the terrain is confined.
Know when the terrain is deadly.

Warring parties must sometimes fight inside their own territory.
This is scattering terrain.

When you enter hostile territory, your penetration is shallow.
This is easy terrain.

Some terrain gives me an advantageous position.
However, it gives others an advantageous position as well.
This will be disputed terrain.

The Work Environment

Use the skills of management.
Know when the work environment is divisive.
Know when the work environment is easy.
Know when the work environment is competitive.
Know when the work environment is open.
Know when the work environment is shared.
Know when the work environment is risky.
Know when the work environment is bad.
Know when the work environment is restricting.
Know when the work environment is do-or-die.

People must sometimes defend their work within the organization.
This is a divisive work environment.

People can address problems with minimum conflict.
This is an easy work environment.

Some work environments are very productive.
These environments also encourage contention.
These are competitive work environments.

The Art of War: Types of Terrain

I can use some terrain to advance easily.
Others, however, can use it to move against me.
This is open terrain.

Everyone shares access to a given area.
The first one there can gather a larger group than anyone else.
This is intersecting terrain.

You can penetrate deeply into hostile territory.
Then many hostile cities are behind you.
This is dangerous terrain.

There are mountain forests.
There are rugged hills.
There are marshes.
Everyone confronts these obstacles on a campaign.
They make bad terrain.

In some areas, the passage is narrow.
You are closed in as you enter and exit them.
In this type of area, a few people can attack our much larger force.
This is confined terrain.

You can sometimes survive only if you fight quickly.
You will die if you delay.
This is deadly terrain.

In some work environments, workers are very productive.
People feel free to criticize each other.
These are open work environments.

Everyone shares access to the same areas and resources.
Those who are better at cooperation will be more productive than others.
This is a shared work environment.

People can be very productive in solving problems.
In doing so, however, they can create enemies.
This is a risky work environment.

There are stupid rules.
There are foolish restrictions.
There are meaningless goals.
Everyone runs into these problems in the organization.
These are bad work environments.

In some organizations, there is little margin for error.
People are locked in once they make a decision.
A small mistake can create big problems for the whole organization.
These are restricting work environments.

Sometimes people can succeed only by committing everything.
They will fail if they delay.
This is a do-or-die work environment.

The Art of War: Types of Terrain

To be successful, you control scattering terrain by not fighting.
Control easy terrain by not stopping.
Control disputed terrain by not attacking.
Control open terrain by staying with the enemy's forces.
Control intersecting terrain by uniting with your allies.
Control dangerous terrain by plundering.
Control bad terrain by keeping on the move.
Control confined terrain by using surprise.
Control deadly terrain by fighting.

Go to any area that helps you in waging war.
You use it to cut off the enemy's contact between his front and back lines.
Prevent his small parties from relying on his larger force.
Stop his strong divisions from rescuing his weak ones.
Prevent his officers from getting his men together.
Chase his soldiers apart to stop them from amassing.
Harass them to prevent their ranks from forming.

When joining battle gives you an advantage, you must do it.
When it isn't to your benefit, you must avoid it.

A daring soldier may ask:
"A large, organized enemy army and its general are coming. What do I do to prepare for them?"

The Art of Management: The Work Environment

To find success in divisive environments, discourage any opposition.
In easy environments, encourage everyone to keep going.
In competitive environments, discourage internal battles.
In open environments, keep everybody working together.
In shared environments, encourage good partnerships.
In risky environments, support the most productive people.
In bad environments, change the rules.
In restricting environments, you must be creative.
In do-or-die environments, encourage your people to succeed.

Identify the most important area for productivity.
You must understand the flow of information between your customers and your organization.
Keep small problems from growing into larger ones.
Keep simple problems from growing into complex ones.
Prevent management problems from affecting employee.
Untangle problems to identify separate issues.
Change procedures to prevent problems from recurring.

If changing the environment benefits you, you must do it.
If changing the environment hurts you, you must avoid it.

You may ask:
"My organization faces very difficult competition. What should I do?"

Tell him:
"First seize an area that the enemy must have.
Then they will pay attention to you.
Mastering speed is the essence of war.
Take advantage of a large enemy's inability to keep up.
Use a philosophy of avoiding difficult situations.
Attack the area where he doesn't expect you."

You must use the philosophy of an invader.
Invade deeply and then concentrate your forces.
This controls your men without oppressing them.

Get your supplies from the riches of the territory.
It is sufficient to supply your whole army.

Take care of your men and do not overtax them.
Your *esprit de corps* increases your momentum.
Keep your army moving and plan for surprises.
Make it difficult for the enemy to count your forces.
Position your men where there is no place to run.
They will then face death without fleeing.
They will find a way to survive.
Your officers and men will fight to their utmost.

Military officers that are completely committed lose their fear.
When they have nowhere to run, they must stand firm.
Deep in enemy territory, they are captives.
Since they cannot escape, they will fight.

There is an answer.
First, protect the most important parts of your organization.
Then your people will pay attention.
Mastering speed is the essence of competition.
Take advantage of a large competitor's inability to keep up.
Your philosophy should be to avoid problem situations.
Target areas that your competitor has overlooked.

You must have an aggressive management philosophy.
Concentrate your organization on being totally competitive.
This commits your people without pressuring them.

You must be productive to succeed in the market.
Only productivity can support your whole organization.

Take care of people and don't overwork them.
Sharing your organization's success verifies your vision.
Keep the organization moving and prepare for surprises.
Make it difficult for the opposition to evaluate you.
Make it difficult for your employees to leave.
They will then face adversity without quitting.
They will find a way to make it work.
Your managers and employees will give it everything they have.

When people are committed, they lose their fear of failure.
When they have nowhere else to go, they stick it out.
Deeply involved in the competition, they are locked in.
When they cannot go elsewhere, they will fight.

Commit your men completely.
Without being posted, they will be on guard.
Without being asked, they will get what is needed.
Without being forced, they will be dedicated.
Without being given orders, they can be trusted.

Stop them from guessing by removing all their doubts.
Stop them from dying by giving them no place to run.

Your officers may not be rich.
Nevertheless, they still desire plunder.
They may die young.
Nevertheless, they still want to live forever.

You must order the time of attack.
Officers and men may sit and weep until their lapels are wet.
When they stand up, tears may stream down their cheeks.
Put them in a position where they cannot run.
They will show the greatest courage under fire.

Make good use of war.
This demands instant reflexes.
You must develop these instant reflexes.
Act like an ordinary mountain snake.
Someone can strike at your head.
You can then attack with your tail
Someone can strike at your tail.
You can then attack with your head.
Someone can strike at your middle.
You can then attack with both your head and tail.

Your people must be totally devoted to their customers.
Without being warned, everyone will defend customers.
Without being asked, everyone will create value.
Without being pushed, they will devote their energy.
Without being directed, they will earn your trust.

Stop their second-guessing by making your commitment clear.
Avoid failure by leaving people no excuses.

Your people and managers may not be rich.
This isn't because they don't want to be wealthy.
They may all fail.
This isn't because they don't want to succeed.

You must establish firm deadlines and targets.
Everyone will complain that they cannot meet them.
They will get working, but they will tell you that it's impossible.
Put them in a position where they have no choice.
They will find a way to make it work.

Make good use of management.
You must make decisions quickly.
Your must develop the ability to decide quickly.
You should be able to act on instinct.
Problems may assail your finances.
Attack with your productivity.
You may have problems with productivity.
Attack these problems with your financial strength.
Problems can occur anywhere.
You must address them immediately.

A daring soldier asks:
"Can any army imitate these instant reflexes?"
We answer:
"It can."

To command and get the most of proud people, you must study adversity.
People work together when they are in the same boat during a storm.
In this situation, one rescues the other just as the right hand helps the left.

Use adversity correctly.
Tether your horses and bury your wagon's wheels.
Still, you can't depend on this alone.
An organized force is braver than lone individuals.
This is the art of organization.
Put the tough and weak together.
You must also use the terrain.

Make good use of war.
Unite your men as one.
Never let them give up.

The commander must be a military professional.
This requires confidence and detachment.
You must maintain dignity and order.
You must control what your men see and hear.
They must follow you without knowing your plans.

You may question:
Can you manage making such quick decisions?
There is only one answer.
You must!

To unite and get the most out of good people, you must have a common enemy.
You must make everyone understand that you are all in the same boat.
All will pull together when your people realize that they are part of a team.

Use adversity correctly.
Tie your people to the success of your organization.
Still, this isn't enough.
A team is stronger than individuals alone.
This is the art of teamwork.
Tie the best people with the weakest.
You must use the best practices.

Make good use of competitive pressure.
Unite your people as one.
Never let them quit.

You must be a management professional.
This requires confidence and detachment.
You must maintain your leadership and focus.
You must control what your people see and hear.
They must believe you without knowing your plans.

You can reinvent your men's roles.
You can change your plans.
You can use your men without their understanding.

You must shift your campgrounds.
You must take detours from the ordinary routes.
You must use your men without giving them your strategy.

A commander provides what his army needs now.
You must be willing to climb high and then kick away your ladder.
You must be able to lead your men deeply into your enemy's territory and then find a way to create the opportunity that you need.

You must drive men like a flock of sheep.

You must drive them to march.
You must drive them to attack.
You must never let them know where you are headed.
You must unite them into a great army.
You must then drive them against all opposition.
This is the job of a true commander.

You must adapt to the different terrain.
You must adapt to find an advantage.
You must manage your people's affections.
You must study all these skills.

You must reinvent your people's job descriptions.
You can change your direction.
You must get the most out of people without them knowing it.

You must change your approach.
You must experiment with different techniques.
You must direct people without explaining your strategy.

You must provide exactly what your people need now.
You must be willing to go out on a limb and take a risk to be successful.
You must get your people deeply involved with the customer to find the problem that creates the opportunity that you need to succeed.

You must inspire people to work together.

You must challenge them to produce.
You must challenge them to improve.
You must never need to explain what your intentions are.
You must unite them into a team.
You must challenge them to beat the opposition.
This is the job of a true manager.

You must adapt to every competitive environment.
You must adjust your methods to succeed.
You must guide your people's emotions.
You must learn all these skills.

Always use the philosophy of invasion.
Deep invasions concentrate your forces.
Shallow invasions scatter your forces.
When you leave your country and cross the border, you must take control.
This is always critical ground.
You can sometimes move in any direction.
This is always intersecting ground.
You can penetrate deeply into a territory.
This is always dangerous ground.
You penetrate only a little way.
This is always easy ground.
Your retreat is closed and the path ahead tight.
This is always confined ground.
There is sometimes no place to run.
This is always deadly ground.

To use scattering terrain correctly, we must inspire our men's devotion.
On easy terrain, we must keep in close communication.
On disputed terrain, we should try to hamper the enemy's progress.
On open terrain, we must carefully defend our chosen position.
On intersecting terrain, we must solidify our alliances.
On dangerous terrain, we must ensure our food supplies.
On bad terrain, we must keep advancing along the road.
On confined terrain, we must barricade a stronghold on the high ground.
On deadly terrain, we must show what we can do by killing the enemy.

You must always manage aggressively.
Commitment to a goal focuses your efforts.
Weak commitments dissipate your efforts.
When you identify a goal and commit to it, you must take control.
This is always a critical environment.
You can sometimes choose different directions.
This is always a good environment for partnerships.
You can commit everything you have to success.
This is always a risky environment.
At the beginning, the investment is small.
This is always an easy environment.
Later, you can't go back and you have few choices.
This is always a restricting environment.
Eventually, you have no place else to go.
This is a do-or-die environment.

To succeed in a divisive work environment, inspire employee dedication.
In an easy work environment, keep in good communication.
In a competitive work environment, you must track everyone's progress.
In an open work environment, everyone must stand behind their work.
In a shared environment, people must work well with others.
In a risky environment, you must have plenty of reserves.
In a bad environment, you must get mistakes behind you.
In a restricting environment, you must protect the organization with visibility.
In a do-or-die environment, everyone must prove themselves by beating the competition.

Make your men feel like an army.
Surround them and they will defend themselves.
If they cannot avoid it, they will fight.
If they are under pressure, they will obey.

Do the right thing when you don't know your different enemies' plans.
Don't attempt to meet them.

You don't know the local mountains, forests, hills and marshes?
Then you cannot march the army.
You don't have local guides?
You won't get any of the benefits of the terrain.

There are many factors in war.
You may lack knowledge of any one of them.
If so, it is wrong to take a nation into war.

You must be able to dominate a nation at war.
Divide a big nation before they are able to gather a large force.
Increase your enemy's fear.
Prevent his forces from getting together and organizing.

Do the right thing and don't try to compete for outside alliances.
You won't have to fight for authority.
Trust only yourself and your own resources.
This increases the enemy's uncertainty.
You can force one of his allies to pull out.
His whole nation can fall.

Make your people feel like a team.
Make them part of the organization and they will defend it.
When they are committed, they will work.
When they are threatened, they will follow your lead.

Do the right thing when you don't understand the work environment.
Don't try to negotiate with people.

What if you don't understand the capacities, boundaries, and limitations?
Then you cannot move the organization.
What if you lack information?
Then you cannot get the benefits of good practices.

There are many issues in management success.
What if you lack understanding of any one of them?
You must not lead an organization in a competitive market.

You must able to control an organization to compete.
Prevent people's work from becoming overwhelming by dividing it.
Increase your opposition's problems.
Prevent the opposition from joining together.

Do the right thing and don't compete by making partnerships with the opponent.
Then you won't have to fight for leadership.
Trust yourself and your own resources.
This increases your opponent's uncertainty.
You may convince your opponents' allies to abandon them.
Then their opposition can collapse.

Distribute plunder without worrying about agreements.
Halt without the government's command.
Attack with the whole strength of your army.
Use your army as if it was a single man.

Attack with skill.
Do not discuss it.
Attack when you have an advantage.
Do not talk about the dangers.
When you can launch your army into deadly ground, even if it stumbles, it can still survive.
You can be weakened in a deadly battle and yet be stronger afterward.

Even a large force can fall into misfortune.
If you fall behind, however, you can still turn defeat into victory.
You must use the skills of war.
To survive, you must adapt to your enemy's purpose.
You must stay with him no matter where he goes.
It may take a thousand miles to kill the general.
If you correctly understand him, you can find the skill to do it.

Manage your government correctly at the start of a war.
Close your borders and tear up passports.
Block the passage of envoys.
Encourage politicians at headquarters to stay out of it.
You must use any means to put an end to politics.
Your enemy's people will leave you an opening.
You must instantly invade through it.

Working alone, you don't have to play politics.
You can change directions without approval.
Focus the entire energy of your organization.
Use your organization as a united force.

Compete with skill.
Don't expose your plans.
Be aggressive when you find an edge.
Don't advertise the risks.
You can get into bad situations and lose a battle, but you can still survive.
You can weaken the organization, but you can also learn from your mistakes.

Even a strong organization can get into trouble.
If you make bad decisions, you can still turn initial failure into ultimate success.
You must use your management skills.
In management, you must adapt completely to the environment.
You must keep up with the competition in every area.
It can take years to win recognition of your leadership.
If you understand the opposition, you can find a way to succeed.

Take the right steps when starting to manage.
Protect your organization and cancel all past privileges.
Get control of the information flow.
Make it clear that you are the person in charge.
Put an end to all office politics.
Identify the critical customer problems that you should solve.
Quickly attack these problems.

Immediately seize a place that they love.
Do it quickly.
Trample any border to pursue the enemy.
Use your judgment about when to fight.

Doing the right thing at the start of war is like approaching a woman.
Your enemy's men must open the door.
After that, you should act like a streaking rabbit.
The enemy will be unable to catch you.

Instantly take control of the work environment.
Waste no time.
Destroy old boundaries to solve customer problems.
Use your best judgement about what to change.

Success at the start of management comes from wooing your people.
The opposition will eventually leave an opening.
When they do, you must act quickly and unpredictably.
Your opponents will be unable to catch up with you.

Attacking with Fire

There are five ways of attacking with fire.
The first is burning troops.
The second is burning supplies.
The third is burning supply transport.
The fourth is burning storehouses.
The fifth is burning camps.

To make fire, you must have the resources.
To build a fire, you must prepare the raw materials.

To attack with fire, you must be in the right season.
To start a fire, you must have the time.

Choose the right season.
The weather must be very dry.

Choose the right time.
Pick a season when the grass is as high as the side of a cart.

You can tell the proper days by the stars in the night sky.
You want days when the wind rises in the morning.

Attacking Cycle Time

There are five ways to shorten cycle time:
First, you can speed production.
Second, you can speed supply.
Third, you can speed delivery.
Fourth, you can eliminate storage.
Fifth, you can speed communication.

To improve cycle time, you must have the proper resources.
To make a change, you must prepare the new procedures.

To improve quickness, you must synchronize processes.
To speed your cycles, you take the time to do it.

Choose the right cycle time.
People must be able to do what is needed.

Choose the right time for change.
Pick a time when the environment is ready.

To know the right time, analyze the use of time.
You want to find time that is currently wasted.

Everyone attacks with fire.
You must create five different situations with fire and be able to adjust to them.

You start a fire inside the enemy's camp.
Then attack the enemy's periphery.

You launch a fire attack, but the enemy remains calm.
Wait and do not attack.

The fire reaches its height.
Follow its path if you can.
If you can't follow it, stay where you are.

Spreading fires on the outside of camp can kill.
You can't always get fire inside the enemy's camp.
Take your time in spreading it.

Set the fire when the wind is at your back.
Don't attack into the wind.
Daytime winds last a long time.
Night winds fade quickly.

Every army must know how to deal with the five attacks by fire.
Use many men to guard against them.

The Art of Management: Attacking Cycle Time

Everyone tries to improve speed.
You must master five different approaches to improving cycle time.

You can directly eliminate certain tasks.
To do this, change the processes around them.

If you eliminate a task, you may have no problems at first.
Wait before making more changes.

The time a job takes expands.
Trace the history of time usage if you can.
If you don't understand it, avoid making changes.

Making small changes outside a process can work.
Don't always eliminate a task; speed it.
Be patient in automating jobs.

Make time cycle changes that other processes support.
Don't save time in one place to lose it in another.
Visible time improvements last a long time.
Subtle ones fade quickly.

You must master these five rules to improve process cycle time.
Use your people to look for new ideas.

When you use fire to assist your attacks, you are being clever.
Water can add force to an attack.
You can also use water to disrupt an enemy.
It doesn't, however, take his resources.

You win in battle by getting the opportunity to attack.
It is dangerous if you fail to study how to accomplish this achievement.
As commander, you cannot waste your opportunities.

We say:
A wise leader plans success.
A good general studies it.
If there is little to be gained, don't act.
If there is little to win, do not use your men.
If there is no danger, don't fight.

As leader, you cannot let your anger interfere with the success of your forces.
As commander, you cannot fight simply because you are enraged.
Join the battle only when it is in your advantage to act.
If there is no advantage in joining a battle, stay put.

Anger can change back into happiness.
Rage can change back into joy.
A nation once destroyed cannot be brought back to life.
Dead men do not return to the living.

When you improve your organization's cycle time, you always create value.
Technology can add force to change.
Using technology can eliminate problems.
It doesn't, however, always create value.

You succeed in any organization by innovating.
It is a mistake if you don't look for opportunities to innovate.
In management, you cannot waste any opportunity.

This much is true.
If you are smart, you plan to succeed.
If you are clever, you examine your organization.
If a change isn't worth the effort, don't attempt it.
If it can't make a difference, don't waste your efforts.
If there is no real problem, you can't solve it.

You must never let your emotions affect the success of your people.
You must never make changes simply because you are angry.
Do only what is needed to make progress.
If there is no benefit in innovation, keep away from it.

Something that upsets you may one day make you happy.
Anger can lead to joy.
If you destroy the organization, there is no second chance.
Fired managers are not rehired.

This fact must make a wise leader cautious.
A good general is on guard.

Your philosophy must be to keep the nation peaceful and the army intact.

Knowing this, you must be careful.
A good manager watches.

Your plan must be to keep the organization together and your people employed.

Using Spies

Altogether, building an army requires thousands of men.
They invade and march thousands of miles.
Whole families are destroyed.
Other families must be heavily taxed.
Every day, thousands of dollars must be spent.

Internal and external events force people to move.
They are unable to work while on the road.
They are unable to find and hold a useful job.
This affects seventy percent of thousands of families.

You can watch and guard for years.
Then a single battle can determine victory in a day.
Despite this, bureaucrats hold onto their salary money too dearly.
They remain ignorant of the enemy's condition.
The result is cruel.

They are not leaders of men.
They are not servants of the state.
They are not masters of victory.

Acquiring Information

Building an economy requires thousands of people.
People labor and work thousands of hours.
They invest a large part of their lives.
Many invest their hard-earned money.
Every day, organizations consume financial resources.

Internal and external events force people to change jobs.
Productivity is lost as they search for work.
Many are unable to find and hold good jobs.
The majority of people have been unemployed at some time.

You can manage an organization for years.
Then a single opportunity can determine success in a day.
Despite this, many managers invest money primarily in salaries.
They don't invest in information.
The result is devastating.

Without information, you cannot manage.
You cannot support your organization.
You cannot be successful.

The Art of War: Using Spies

You need a creative leader and a worthy commander.
You must move your troops to the right places to beat others.
You must accomplish your attack and escape unharmed.
This requires foreknowledge.
You can obtain foreknowledge.
You can't get it from demons or spirits.
You can't see it from professional experience.
You can't check it with analysis.
You can only get it from other people.
You must always know the enemy's situation.

You must use five types of spies.
You need local spies.
You need inside spies.
You need double agents.
You need doomed spies.
You need surviving spies.

You need all five types of spies.
No one must discover your methods.
You will be then able to put together a true picture.
This is the commander's most valuable resource.

You need local spies.
Get them by hiring people from the countryside.

You need inside spies.
Win them by subverting government officials.

You need double agents.
Discover enemy agents and convert them.

You must be a creative and productive manager.
You must put your resources in the right places to be productive.
You must survive in a competitive environment.
This requires information.
You can get this information.
You won't get it from theory.
You won't get it from past experience.
You can't reason it out.
You can only get it by collecting it from other people.
You must always know your organization's condition.

You must use five types of information.
You need process information.
You need personnel information.
You need competitor information.
You need market information.
You need customer information.

You must use all five types of information.
If you do, no one can challenge your knowledge.
You can monitor your organization and its workings.
Information is your most valuable resource.

You need information on your processes.
Win it by putting measuring systems into place.

You need information on your people.
Find out what people can do through regular evaluations.

You need information on competitive methods.
Hire people from other organizations and use them.

You need doomed spies.
Deceive professionals into being captured.
We let them know our orders.
They then take those orders to our enemy.

You need surviving spies.
Someone must return with a report.

Your job is to build a complete army.
No relations are as intimate as they are with spies.
No rewards are too generous for spies.
No work is as secret as that of spies.

If you aren't clever and wise, you can't use spies.
If you aren't fair and just, you can't use spies.
If you can't see the tiny subtleties, you won't get the truth from spies.

Pay attention to small, trifling details!
Spies are helpful in every area.

Spies are the first to hear information, so they must not spread it.
Spies who give your location or talk to others must be killed along with those to whom they have talked.

You need market information.
You need to know where to obtain the best prices.
Let the market know your needs.
Encourage bidding to decrease your costs.

You need customer information.
You must know what your customers think.

Your job is to develop a strong organization.
No resources are as critical as information sources.
No reward is too generous for good information.
No knowledge is as hard to win as timely information.

You must be smart enough to correlate data.
You must be open and unbiased to evaluate it.
If you aren't sensitive to subtleties, you won't find the truth in information.

You must pay close attention to small details.
Information is helpful in every area.

Your people must gather information, but they must not spread it.
People that divulge your processes or plans to opponents can destroy you.

The Art of War: Using Spies

You may want to attack an army's position.
You may want to attack a certain fortification.
You may want to kill people in a certain place.
You must first know the guarding general.
You must know his left and right flanks.
You must know his hierarchy.
You must know the way in.
You must know where different people are stationed.
We must demand this information from our spies.

I want to know the enemy spies in order to convert new spies into my men.
You find a source of information and bribe them.
You must bring them in with you.
You must obtain them as double agents and use them as your emissaries.

Do this correctly and carefully.
You can contact both local and inside spies and obtain their support.
Do this correctly and carefully.
You create doomed spies by deceiving professionals.
You can use them to give false information.
Do this correctly and carefully.
You must have surviving spies capable of bringing you information at the right time.

You may want to copy your competitor's best practices.
You may want to create a new department.
You may want to close an existing department.
You must first know how the opposition thinks.
You must know how others are organized.
You must know unofficial hierarchies.
You must know where opportunities are.
You must know where people want to work.
You must get this information from people.

You want to know who understand competitor's practices and hire them.
You must be willing to pay for information.
You must attract knowledgeable people to you.
You must win people with outside experience and use them to attract others.

You must do this carefully.
You can hire from your competitors and win their knowledge.
You must also do this selectively.
You can discover purchasing information from the market.
You can use market competition to get better prices.
You must do this quietly as well.
You need detailed information on customer satisfaction at all times.

The Art of War: Using Spies

These are the five different types of intelligence work.
You must be certain to master them all.
You must be certain to create double agents.
You cannot afford to be too cheap in creating these double agents.

This technique created the success of ancient emperors.
This is how they held their dynasties.

You must always be careful of your success.
Learn from the past examples.

Be a smart commander and good general.
You do this by using your best and brightest people for spying.
This is how you achieve the greatest success.
This is how you meet the necessities of war.
The whole army's position and ability to move depends on these spies.

There are five different types of information.
You must be certain to get access to them all.
You must be certain to understand competitive practices.
You cannot invest too much time in understanding the best practices.

This is how managers create successful organizations.
This is how they have been successful.

You must always be careful of your success.
Learn from the history of success.

You must be an informed and capable manager.
You must use your best and brightest people to gather information.
This is how you achieve the greatest success.
This is how you satisfy the needs of the organization.
Your management practices and ability to produce depends on information.

Winning Markets

The Art of War & The Art of Marketing takes Sun Tzu's lessons and helps you use them to identify markets, position against the competition, and win battles in the marketplace. You can almost directly apply the lessons of *The Art of War* to the marketing of your company and its products. *The Art of Marketing* gives you Sun Tzu's ideas in a form that addresses the strategic issues of competition in today's terminology.

Like *The Art of War & The Art of Management*, you get both books side-by-side. You get our translation of *The Art of War.* Additionally, you get Sun Tzu's ideas interpreted line-by-line to help you win the real-world battles in the marketplace.

The Art of War & The Art of Marketing deals with the external issues of winning customer awareness and generating sales. In many ways, it is the perfect companion book to *The Art of Management,* the book you currently hold in your hand, which focuses on the internal organization. Using them together, you can address both the internal and external concerns of your organization.

The Art of War & The Art of Marketing
ISBN: 1929194021
Paperback. $14.95.

Clearbridge Publishing books may be purchased for business, for any promotional use, or for special sales. Please contact:

Clearbridge Publishing
Phone: (206) 533-9357
Fax: (206) 546-9756
Mail: P.O. Box 7055, Shoreline, WA 98133
E-mail: info@clearbridge.com.
Web: www.clearbridge.com

For Sales Professionals

The Art of War & The Art of Sales takes Sun Tzu's lessons and shows you how to specifically apply them to today's problems of contacting customers, convincing them to buy, and winning their on-going business. If you are responsible for sales or sales management, you will want this version of *The Art of War* written to address the needs of individual sales people fighting for orders from buyers. If you manage a sales force, you will want to buy this version of Sun Tzu for your people to study.

Like *The Art of War & The Art of Management*, you get two books side-by-side. You get our translation of *The Art of War*. Additionally, you get Sun Tzu's ideas interpreted line-by-line to help working sales professionals in the battle for sales. If you are a sales manager or company president, you will be more than happy with the results of your sales people following Sun Tzu's advice. This is a book they will read and a philosophy they will use. The enemy is the competition. The battleground is the customer's mind. Victory is winning an on-going relationship with the customer. The two versions are shown side-by-side to give you a complete picture of using Sun Tzu's approach to modern selling.

The Art of War & The Art of Sales
ISBN: 1929194013
Paperback. $14.95.

Clearbridge Publishing books may be purchased for business, for any promotional use, or for special sales. Please contact:

Clearbridge Publishing
Phone: (206) 533-9357
Fax: (206) 546-9756
Mail: P.O. Box 7055, Shoreline, WA 98133
E-mail: info@clearbridge.com.
Web: www.clearbridge.com

Discover the Original Text
with each Chinese Ideogram Translated

Would you like to read the real *Art of War*? Sun Tzu originally wrote his text in Chinese characters or ideograms. Any English translation is only an approximation of Sun Tzu's original ideas. However, you can now easily read and appreciate Sun Tzu's text in its original form. *The Art of War: In Sun Tzu's Own Words* is the only book to give you Sun Tzu's Chinese text as he originally wrote it. You can see both a character-by-character translation as well as a line-by-line translation of his ideas into English.

This book gives you two different versions. Uniquely, it gives you Sun Tzu's original Chinese ideograms translated one at a time in the phrases he actually used. You see these characters and their translation on the left-hand page. On the right-hand page, you can see how the groups of original characters in *The Art of War* are translated into English sentences. The two versions are shown side-by-side to give you a complete picture of the Sun Tzu's original lessons on warfare. You will find the original Chinese both more subtle and suggestive than the English version.

The Art of War: In Sun Tzu's Own Words
ISBN: 1929194005
Paperback. $9.95.

Clearbridge Publishing books may be purchased for business, for any promotional use, or for special sales. Please contact:

Clearbridge Publishing
Phone: (206) 533-9357
Fax: (206) 546-9756
Mail: P.O. Box 7055, Shoreline, WA 98133
E-mail: info@clearbridge.com
Web: www.clearbridge.com